THE HEART-CONNECTED LIFE...
...for parents

Raising God-Dependent Teens

Susan Cottrell

Copyright © 2009 by Susan Cottrell

THE HEART-CONNECTED LIFE...*for parents*
by Susan Cottrell

Printed in the United States of America

ISBN 978-1-60791-201-9

All rights reserved solely by the author. The author guarantees all contents are original and do not infringe upon the legal rights of any other person or work. No part of this book may be reproduced in any form without the permission of the author. The views expressed in this book are not necessarily those of the publisher.

Scripture taken from the NEW AMERICAN STANDARD BIBLE®, Copyright © 1960,1962,1963,1968,1971,1972,1973,1975, 1977,1995 by The Lockman Foundation. Used by permission.

www.xulonpress.com

*To Mr. Wonderful, the best parent I've ever known.
Our children are beyond blessed to call you Daddy.*

contents

the heart of parenting

1 Start with the Heart	8
2 What's The Goal?	14
3 Good, Evil and Life	22
4 They're Going to Look Like You	34
5 Out of Control	42

whose journey is it?

6 Scope and Sequence	54
7 God Bless the Broken Road	66
8 Respecting Their Journey	74
9 Man Looks at the Outward Appearance	84
10 Loving the Prodigal	92

what's a parent to do?

11 Delight in Them (As God Delights in Us)	106
12 Encouragement – The Gift that Keeps on Giving	112
13 Respect versus Shame	118
14 Guide Them (As God Guides)	124
15 Guys, Girls and Sexual Identity	130
16 Dating and Sexuality	136

staying heart-connected

17 Power of God Trumps the Law   148
18 Thank God Almighty We Are Free At Last   154

acknowledgements

Writing a book seems like a solitary endeavor, but many people helped bring this book about. Thank you to those who read and edited, to those who believed in and encouraged me, to those who generously prayed, and to my children who said to each other, "Shh, Mom's working!" Simply know that I could not have done it without you.

Leslie Martin, Tracy Munsil and Shelley Olson, thank you for editing, for encouraging and for seeing what I could not see. Denise Cromer, Chris Holly and Tabitha Warnica, thank you for believing in me. And thank you to Elijah Amman, Larry Hughes and Veronica Martinez for final editing. (It's tough to get an error-free book!) Micheal Wells, thank you for generously sharing what God is teaching you.

Lauren Lankford, thank you for the beautiful cover art.

Thank you to Mr. Wonderful, who has nurtured all of my dreams, and without whom life would not be nearly as much fun!

And Lord, for the intimate loving relationship You have given me, I can never fully express my delight. You breathed this book through me and allowed me to put my name on it. I love You.

the heart of parenting

chapter 1
START WITH THE HEART

> *"We know the truth, not only by the reason, but also by the heart."* Blaise Pascal

> *"Create a taste for God in the heart of your child and when he is old, nothing else will satisfy."* Paraphrase of Proverbs 22:6, source unknown

> *"The mind can't take you where your heart longs to go."* Unknown

What is Heart-Connected Life?

When I was young, my heart's desire was to marry somebody wonderful and have children. Parenting was a soft-focus image of brushing my daughters' long silky hair, enjoying intellectual family dinner conversations, and reading beautiful literature to my children as they lay under blankets by the fire.

I discovered that the reality is not the dream.

Once I actually had kids, this was the picture: I explode in anger over a mild inconvenience; I am far more selfish than I thought; and for my precious child to scream, *No!* – or lie to my face – upsets me more than I thought possible. And who factored in the cooking, cleaning and laundry?

So here I am writing a parenting book!

You see, in these twenty-some years of parenting, God has grown me up. He has softened the edge of my anger; he has made me less selfish, and he has brought me to an intimate and loving relationship not only with Him but with my children. We are not a perfect family, but we are a healthy family. (It is only after giving up the image of a perfect family is it *possible* to be a healthy family.) I have learned many things at His hand that I would like to share, that I hope will encourage you.

I am trained in lay counseling, and I have counseled women and teens. Teens have lived with us for periods when they have been unable to live at home. I did not know how much I loved teens until God grew me through my own teens and the extra ones He put in my life. He has shown me that in relating to teens (or anyone), *nothing* is more important than for hearts to be connected.

God has led me over some rough terrain to develop this work: The Heart-Connected Life.

I grew up in a home where religion was ridiculed, and though I attended the occasional Sunday school class at a tender age, my parents were not Christian. The years after my mother died (I was nine) were marked by my father's open hostility to anything religious. But the years of violence and abuse notwithstanding, God accepted me as His child. Three important truths have emerged for me from this background.

First, God seeks us out. I was very young when He drew me to Himself, giving me the desire to pray and read Psalms. God personally sought me out and revealed Himself to me. I knew that God loved me and that I could interact with Him authentically and unashamedly. I later learned from the Bible that we love because He first loved us, and that while we are going our merry way, He draws us – calling us by name and seeking a love relationship. Had He not been calling me those long and confusing years, I would not have stood a chance.

This leads to the second truth, that nothing can thwart God's plan. He will reveal Himself to us through our fallen lives – including a dysfunctional family. I might easily have fallen through the cracks. But God's plan is not thwarted, and despite it all, He saved me. We can take courage in God's great sovereignty over our children, and not be afraid for them. Whatever responsibility we have to our children, we are primarily responsible to hear God and follow Him. *He* is sovereign over them. What a relief!

The third vital truth is that the trappings of church are not the same as a relationship with God. My own relationship with Jesus is not mixed with memories of sitting in pews, passing a plate or singing hymns. These are not wrong things, but they are not the same as knowing God personally. Countless Christians the world over, throughout history, have known God intimately without any of this.

Jesus is about the heart

Once, as young Christians, my husband and I were rehearsing music with the young piano player from our church. He began playing an old hymn that we didn't know. "You don't know *that*?" he said. "What kind of church did you grow up in?!"

I answered: "We didn't grow up in church!"

Christ is not the same as "Christianity." I have learned to focus on the simplicity and centrality of Christ (2 Corinthians 11:3). While growing up in a non-Christian home carries grave dangers, knowing Him apart from the trappings of religion is an inestimable advantage.

These truths have given me a heart-knowledge that wild horses could not drag out of me: Jesus is about the heart. Nowhere do we see Jesus focus on appearance, words, behavior, obedience or anything except as they issue from the heart. He does not focus on the fruit; He waters the tree and the fruit comes. Everything Jesus ever did shows us that the heart is what matters. He let a woman go who had been caught in adultery (John 8:11). But he lambasts a church leader for asking a question (Matthew 16:1-4). "As a man thinks in his heart, so is he" (Proverbs 23:7).

Jesus offers to restore our heart, give us a new heart, and indwell our heart. The more deeply I know Him, the more He shows me that *all of life* issues from the heart. And so God brought forth in me *The Heart-Connected Life*.

Our heart connected to God, to our redeemed selves, and to our loved ones, is what makes life worth the living. Getting our heart connected is the path to maturity, to joy, to Christ-likeness. This journey in parenting is about getting our heart connected to our children – and seeing their hearts connected to God. "Watch over your heart with all diligence, for from it flow the springs of life" (Proverbs 4:23). Parenting begins with the heart.

This book is designed to connect you with your teens at the heart level, and God has a plan to do that in each of us with our kids. The "to-do list" approach is insufficient to the challenges facing our teens today.

A recent article said this about window treatments: "Window treatments must let in light, but keep out the harsh sun. They must allow us a view, but maintain our privacy. They must be beautiful, but not attract attention. They should look rich, but be easy to keep clean. They also have to be affordable and come in the right colors. We expect a lot from our window treatments!" Who knew?

We also expect a lot from our teens. They are no longer kids but not yet grownups. They need to show responsibility but they don't get full privileges. They are dealing with adult hormones and physical changes, but they better not act on them! They can drive to pick up a younger sibling from a late event, but they can't keep the car out late to hang out with friends. We want them to show mature judgment in making decisions, though they've never yet made such decisions. We want them to learn from their mistakes, but we prefer they not make mistakes! They need to

> "Basically, the idea is, 'make us proud, but be low maintenance.'"

get an education to prepare for adulthood, though most of what they're learning is of little or no interest to them! They need to grapple through their thoughts with a mature adult, but most of what they talk about is of little or no interest to us (when we're at our worst).

As I said, we expect a lot of our teens.

My interior designer sister summed up the window-treatments philosophy thus: "Basically, the idea is, 'make us proud, but be low maintenance.'" Perhaps that is our wish for parenting, too!

In my years of parenting and counseling teens, God has shown me that it's all about the heart (theirs *and* ours). Isn't the same true with evangelism, with discipling, with marriage? As you read through the Bible, you see that *Jesus* is about the heart. Jesus always addresses the heart because the heart is what He came for, and because obedience without the heart is just self-will.

If you are viewing the teen years as overwhelming, don't despair! This may look like the mystery of the ages – like an alien has taken over your wonderful kid – but that's not true. My hope is for you to discover that you love teens; I am trusting God to do something miraculous.

Some concepts will be quite new to you, and some you've just forgotten. Give yourself time to grow. Think of it this way: you have gotten a haircut, your stylist has done a great job with it, and it looks fantastic. But when you try to style it, it won't work. Why is she able to do it and you are not? It's not even her hair!! Because she works with hair every single day, all types of hair, and she knows hair. But if you play around with it until you get used to it, you will find it's not as hard as you think.

So I encourage you to work with the concepts in this book until you get used to them – and let the Lord reveal to you – because it's not as hard as you think.

My approach is to look at how God parents us. We'll be taking some hard looks at our beliefs, and the first few chapters will lay a foundation. This isn't a "list of problems and the answers to go with them" (though this may answer many questions). It is more about how God interacts with us, and how we can interact with our kids.

Heartwork

The following are questions for you to ask God in your personal time with Him.
1. How did He first draw your heart to Him?
2. How did you imagine parenting would be?
3. Where the reality has fallen short of the image?
4. What trappings of the church have you believed to be vital that are not vital?
5. Where has your heart known Him and loved Him, separate from your actions?
6. Where has your heart held back from Him, not trusted Him, if only in a small thing?
7. In what ways does He want you to trust Him?
8. What expectations have you had of your children?
9. What else He would like to show you now?

• • •

chapter 2
WHAT'S THE GOAL?

> *"I press on toward the goal for the prize of the upward call of God in Christ Jesus."* Philippians 3:14

> *"But the goal of our instruction is love from a pure heart and a good conscience and a sincere faith."* 1 Timothy 1:5

> *"If you don't change your course, you're likely to end up where you're headed."* Unknown

Where are we Headed?

Goal setting is not my thing. I'm more likely to shoot from the hip. But we have to know the city we're traveling to in order to get on the right train. And if we want to be satisfied with our job of parenting, it helps to know what we can expect and, more importantly, what we cannot.

What are our goals as parents? Consider your desires for your teens and how you want them to be equipped when they leave home. You may be able to summarize your goals for your kids, or those goals may be hazy. Either way, our goals drive us, conscious or not, so let's consider these common goals and possible motives.

Obedience. We want kids to be obedient for their own good. It serves them to follow authority because they will have to do it all their lives. But, if we're honest, we also want obedience because it makes us look good.

Purity. Scripture is clear about purity, and we have seen the wreckage from promiscuity. We surely want to spare our kids that heartache (*and danger*) if possible.

Godliness/holiness. That sounds very good, and scripture tells us to be holy. But what exactly does that mean and how do we achieve it? One person's holiness is not another's (Is a missionary more holy than a singer? Not if both are following God's lead. Or is it more holy to go to church than to read a book? It all depends on God's leading. We'll see that more as we go.)

Education. A good education is practical, perhaps indispensable, and it paves the way to achieving dreams. But our kids' good education also does "good" for us. I mean, who doesn't want whiz kids? Whose chest doesn't swell when Junior gets straight A's or cures cancer? (My father's identity was wrapped up in his exceptional intelligence. What do you think it did to him that his firstborn son was mentally handicapped?)

Substance-free. We could weep at the destruction drugs have caused in this generation of teens. Drugs are readily available, and like satan's lies, they offer the world but deliver death. But the teens (or adults) I have seen succumb to drugs have been seeking to meet a need in their heart. Addressing those needs seems key to avoiding this pit.

Are you like me in thinking these goals can be confusing, even overwhelming? We are not sure how to achieve them, and at this point, we may not even be sure which ones are worth shooting for. It's easy to withdraw, to say, "I can't do it." Or worse, we turn up the heat and "straighten those kids out." But both options lead to a fractured relationship. Instead, let's drill down to the core.

Our Greatest Parenting Goal

As I was praying through this book, the Lord simplified it for me to one overriding principle.

Matthew 22:36-40 says: "'Teacher, which is the great commandment in the Law?' And He said to him, '*You shall love the Lord your God with all your heart, and with all your soul, and with all your mind.'* This is the great and foremost commandment. The second is like it, *'You shall love your neighbor as yourself.'* On these two commandments depend the whole Law and the Prophets."

Mark adds: *"(This) is much more than all burnt offerings and sacrifices."* Mark 12:33.

So loving God with everything in you, and loving your neighbor as yourself, this greatest commandment, sums up the law and the prophets. This is more than all the burnt offerings and sacrifices. Look at all the pages from Genesis to Malachi, and know that Jesus has summed them all up right here. Isn't that remarkable? This is the heart-connected life God had been showing me. As Jesus said this is the most important thing, it seems we are wise to start here with our kids.

All my parenting experience comes down to this great commandment, and anything that we desire for our children will flow out of it. So much is packed into this great truth, we will spend the book unpacking it.

By "loving God," Jesus was talking about the polar opposite of the law, from which we have been freed in Him. God has used my years of parenting, counseling and observation, to show me *loving Him* in practice. It was in Jesus' words all along, but I didn't experience it until I saw it in the trenches.

It's Not About the Law

Early in my parenting, I experienced something magnificent that showed me that the law is incomplete. My five kids were ages eight down to newborn. Being a sanguine personality, I have never run a very tight ship. A friend gave me some tapes about getting your baby on a schedule, which helped me a lot. The tapes also talked about other things - teaching kids respect, first-time obedience, and other principles. I was homeschooling all these kids, and I thought, *I could use a tighter ship!* So I began down this path, and I made progress. But after a while, it didn't work so well. We began to get weighed down, and we weren't having much fun. My husband Rob, knowing my inconsistent personality, said, "Just stick with the tapes. Follow what they're saying." I did. But it wasn't working.

> That's what legalism is: following a regimen to produce a desired result, rather than listening to the Lord's leading and letting *Him* produce the result.

I went to a ladies' retreat and as it happened, I took a long walk with the pastor's wife. I began telling her about this dilemma of mine, that the tapes were not working as they had been, and I asked for her advice. She suggested I had become legalistic, but that didn't make sense to me. I understood a legalist as being a high-strung rule-follower, and I am certainly not that type. I'm the shoot-from-the-hip type.

Then she showed me how I was looking to the to-do list on these tapes to produce a certain result. That's what legalism is: following a regimen to produce a desired result, rather than listening to the Lord's leading and letting Him produce the result. The expectation, "Do *this* to produce *that*," is a lie.

God gave her that insight for me. I had not yet run this by Rob, and on the way home, I prayed that if this was really from the Lord, He would prepare Rob to hear, and he and I would come to agreement.

When I told Rob all about my conversation, he said that I should throw the tapes out. What a relief! He understood and agreed. How sweetly God confirmed this direction for us. This became a turning point for us to parent according to the Lord's leading, and not by the to-do list. We had already learned to hear the Lord's voice. But the lure of the to-do-list parenting is strong, because it promises well-trained kids who love the Lord. But it doesn't deliver. We had much more growth ahead of us, of course, but this watershed event showed me that my children's growth is not my job; it's Jesus' job. My job is to keep turning them to

Him, until they accept Him as their Savior, and then to continue to turn them to Him as their Savior, as He becomes their all-in-all. It makes parenting remarkably simple.

A good analogy is evangelism: our job is not to lead people to the Lord, but to respond as the Lord directs us and then watch *Him* draw them. (John 6:44: "No one can come to Me unless the Father who sent Me draws him.") I can't get anyone to accept the Lord! I can't even convict anyone of their need for Him... and I'm wrong to try. But I can respond to the Lord who *will* lead them. No pastor gets anyone to accept Christ as their Savior; he offers the invitation, in obedience, and God draws them.

Their response to Christ does not determine whether we were right to share. We are right to follow the Lord's leading and let Him produce the increase. It's the same with our kids.

Lead Them to Their Savior

Let's turn back to Jesus' great commandment, which I consider our goal in parenting. To put it another way, our goal is to lead our children toward Christ until they come to know Him for themselves as their initial Savior, and then continue to point them to Him as they learn to abide in Him fully for themselves as their ongoing Savior. That means not only to lead them to Christ until they come to their own salvation experience, but to continually point them back to Him as they come to depend on Him more and more. Issues of their hearts, direction in their lives, and answers to their problems, all come down to trusting Him as their Savior - not only to lead them to conversion, but throughout their ongoing journey, as they live, grow and mature in Him. We have some eighteen years to show them that nothing will be more important than depending on their Savior for their very life and breath and being. Everything else flows from that.

It Starts With Us

On this parenting journey, *we* are called on to demonstrate our own relationship to the Lord, living in Him authentically and transparently, because that kind of intimacy cannot be faked, especially with these people who see us at our worst! "Do as I say, not as I do" does not work; they will grow in the Lord *not* because we tell them to but because they see it in us.

Think about the person who led you to the Lord. What was it that drew you: their words or their being? I love 2 Corinthians 2:14: "But thanks be to God, who always leads us in triumph in Christ, and manifests through us the sweet aroma of the knowledge of Him in every place." It was the sweet aroma of Christ in my sister that drew me to Him. A baker doesn't have to explain the aroma of freshly baked bread - the aroma alone draws them. And anyone who walks in the bakery will smell it in the air.

The aroma of Christ will be in us as we grow in Him. I've felt that I've grown more in this parenting process than my kids! Some years ago, my friend was very attentive to every detail of her only child's development: *Is she polite? Is she other-focused? Is she using her God-given talents?* But she confessed that this attentiveness was driving her daughter crazy! I suggested she not focus so much on all these details but instead focus on the Lord and how He is growing her as a mom. She did. And as she grew, her daughter naturally bloomed right in her wake.

We get eighteen years for this job because of all the on-the-job training that's required - allowing plenty of time for mistakes, false starts and rabbit trails. God has a lot of patience in teaching us how to parent our children!

Our goal as parents is simple. But it's not simplistic. Our job as parents is simple. But it's not easy.

In Matthew 11:28-29, Jesus says: "Come to Me, all who are weary and heavy-laden, and I will give you rest. Take My yoke upon you and learn from Me, for I am gentle and humble in heart, and you will find rest for your souls." If two oxen are harnessed together pulling a plow, both are going to pull pretty evenly. But if a 200-pound man is on one side and a little boy is on the other, who will be doing the work? I don't think the boy will do any work at all. It won't be difficult for him because he's going to be carried along by the man! And the man will be happy to do it, because although the boy is willing, he doesn't have the capacity to pull the plow.

How much more does Jesus do all the work when we get in the yoke with Him? We need only stay in the yoke; He will do the work through us. If I am struggling to pull this plow, I'm not finding rest for my soul. I find rest because the plow is being pulled for me while I am resting my soul in Him.

Don't be fooled into thinking we are being lazy or passive because we let Him pull the plow. Is it lazy to allow God to right a situation where I have been wronged? No. It takes all my restraint! Am I lazy to allow God to work on my child over time when I want to whip her into shape? No. It takes constant dependence on Him. But these things finally lead to rest. Jesus tells us to rest and to cast our cares upon Him.

Conclusion

What do you want at the end of your parenting tenure? Do you want to make decisions for your son at thirty that you made for him at three? No. So how do you get from here to there? Do you want to make decisions for your daughter until she's married? Do you want to be good friends with your kids when they're grown? What do you want to be left with? I hope you find it incredibly freeing to see that you are fully equipped *in Christ* to do an amazing job parenting your kids.

> Jesus said, "Follow Me." If we follow Him, He will lead us wherever we need to go.

If we stay with our guiding principle of fully loving God and others, our Savior will teach us more than we teach our kids! He will tenderly show us where we are not abiding in Him, where we are not trusting Him. And we will shift from behavior modification to growing kids whose *heart* is in Christ, kids who love God with all their heart. That is where we - and our kids - come alive!

I hope all this resonates in your soul, and that the Spirit is affirming it in you. Jesus said, "I came that you may have life, and have it abundantly" (John 10:10). If the Spirit is telling you, *Yes, this is from Me*, then it will be a matter of letting Him show you what it all means.

Parenting kids is about the heart. It is not about good ideas or even about behavior. It is about hearing God, and letting everything flow from that. Jesus said, "Follow Me." If we follow Him, He will lead us wherever we need to go. Parenting is no different from living the Christian life, except for the kids involved!

In the next chapter we will discover something huge about rules and why we are obsessed with them - as well as why they don't work. We are also going to see that we were *never meant* to focus on rules.

Heartwork

1. Ask God to show you what is working for you in parenting.
2. Ask Him to show you what is not working.
3. Ask Him to show you what goals you have been seeking to achieve with your kids.
4. Ask Him to show you His goals for you as a parent and for your teen.
5. What is God's plan for your relationship with Him?
6. What is God showing you in this chapter?

• • •

chapter 3
GOOD, EVIL AND LIFE

> *"Law itself will not maintain an orderly society without an internal moral code."* George Washington

> *"We are sometimes more religious than Jesus Himself. I wonder - would he be uncomfortable in our churches?"* Rob Whittaker, Principal of Capernwray Bible College

> *"Jesus does not offer to make bad people good but to make dead people alive."* Ravi Zacharias

We're going to dig into some deep theology, questioning ideas you may have believed for a long time. But it is necessary to live the kind of abundant life Jesus offers, and to see how God really wants us to relate to Him and to our teens.

I am reminded of a friend who, at age forty, went to the doctor for her painful, aching feet. Her toes were becoming deformed, and she had trouble walking. He discovered the problem readily: her shoes were too small - *by a full size*. This is a true story! That's good news, because it was easy to fix - without surgery. But that's bad news, because she had to buy all new shoes - cha-ching. Why were all her shoes so small? Because she said as she grew to a size 10, she was reluctant to admit her foot had grown to a size 11! So, I hope you can see that a small mental block, or false belief, can affect our whole "walk" (ha ha). As we work through this, listen to what the Lord may be telling you, even if it feels as if He's asking you to try on bigger shoes.

The Lists

Draw a circle with a vertical line through it. Write "Do" on one side and "Don't" on the other side. We can list some things right now with very little thought. Try it.

Do:
Read our Bible
Pray
Give money to missionaries
Go to church
Teach our kids
Love each other

Don't:
Kill people
Disobey God
Blaspheme God
Swear
Hate

Okay, good. It comes pretty easily, doesn't it?

Do you think most people have these Do/Don't lists? Do Baptists have their Do/Don't lists? Do Methodists? Mormons? Jehovah's Witnesses? Buddhists? Muslims? Believers and non-believers? Yes. All of them have their Do/Don't lists. These lists come easily to all of us. It's very human.

Now, draw a big circle around the lists like a treetop, and put a trunk on it. What have we got now? The tree of the knowledge of good and evil. Do you see that? We just came up with our own knowledge of what's good and evil, didn't we?

But as you can see from Genesis 2, God warns us not to live off that tree. He was very clear about that. Genesis 2:16-17 says: "The LORD God commanded the man, saying, 'From any tree of the garden you may eat freely; but from the tree of the knowledge of good and evil you shall not eat, for in the day that you eat from

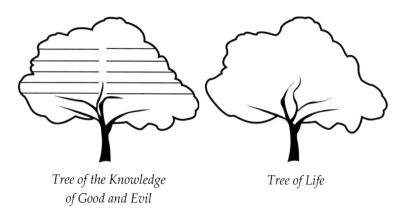

Tree of the Knowledge of Good and Evil

Tree of Life

> God never wanted us to be determining good and evil.

it you will surely die.'"

After Eve tells the serpent that they will die if they eat from the tree of knowledge, it says this in Genesis 3:4: "Then the serpent said to the woman, 'You surely will not die. For God knows that in the day you eat from it your eyes will be opened, and you will be like God, knowing good and evil.'"

You see, satan tempted Adam and Eve to think that they would be as wise as God if they ate from the tree of knowledge - that God was holding something back from them (instead of protecting them). You know what? God never wanted us to be determining good and evil. That is why He said, "Don't eat from the tree of the knowledge of good and evil." If He had *wanted* us deciding what's good and what's evil, He could have taught us that. We're intelligent. He could have shown us. But with the knowledge of good and evil comes the responsibility of deciding good and evil that we're not equipped for. That's the problem. We don't think about that part. With the knowledge of good and evil comes living independent of God. That is why it is not called the tree of good and evil - because it's the *knowledge* of good and evil that gets us into trouble. It means that *we* are deciding what is good and what is evil.

Who decides what's right or wrong for God? Only God. He has no higher source than Himself to determine right and wrong. When we begin to decide what is good and evil, we have no higher source than ourselves to determine right and wrong. So we're acting like God. This tree stands for autonomy, independence and self-rule. God does not want us deciding what's good and evil. (I know we can support any decision of something being good or evil with the Bible, but so could the Pharisees, and Jesus did not appreciate their evaluations.)

God wants us eating from the tree of life - which is Jesus. He is the Way, the Truth and the Life. He wants us to rely solely on Him for our life, not on our own knowledge. The tree of life (Jesus) stands for life (union with God) versus death (separation from God). When you eat from the tree of life, you settle matters of good and evil *relationally*, with God. When you eat from the tree of knowledge, you settle matters of good and evil from the Do/Don't list - or *legalistically*.

Here's how this relates to those teens of ours. We are responsible to make decisions for them daily, and our natural tendency is to make those decisions from the tree of knowledge. And the more we make those decisions from the tree of knowledge, the more likely our children will rebel in unfathomable ways.

I have known quite a few families with impossibly high standards for their children. The following story is a fictionalized composite, but a realistic representation of these families.

John and Jane Doe did everything by the book for their children: strict church, old-fashioned virtue studies with the daughters and knighthood studies with the sons. Their picture should have been on the cover of a Christian magazine. But the strictures were too tight. The oldest son left home and never looked back; the oldest daughter became pregnant at sixteen, and the next daughter became addicted to crystal meth. Who would have predicted it? What happened between those little children sitting at the table reading Proverbs, and these teens they hardly recognize? Here is what happened: the parents made their decisions from the tree of knowledge instead of from the tree of life.

Genesis 3:22-23 (after Adam and Eve have eaten from the tree of knowledge) reads: "Then the Lord God said, 'Look, the human beings have become like us, knowing both good and evil. What if they reach out, take fruit from the tree of life, and eat it? Then they will live forever!' So the Lord God banished them from the Garden of Eden, and he sent Adam out to cultivate the ground from which he had been made" (NLT).

Why did God close off access to the tree of life? Because He did *not* want them living eternally in the state of knowledge of good and evil, which means independence from God. Before the tree of knowledge, Adam and Eve simply depended on God. They found out from Him what to do and where to go. They enjoyed communion with Him. But once they started deciding what was good or evil, it all changed.

Now, we're going to take a tiny detour for this question: why would you let your preschooler help you make cookies? I mean, she wouldn't be any help. If you did it, you would make the cookies in half the time and a fourth the mess. So why do you do it? It's not to train her. Start her at ten and she'll do fine. There's only one reason to let your preschooler help you: relationship. We do it for the relationship.

Why does God let us "help" Him? Why does He give us a part in humanity, in teaching, in evangelizing? For the relationship. He does not need us. You've heard the little sentiment: "God made mothers because He couldn't be everywhere at once!" I know that's just an encouragement to mothers, to make us feel needed! But it's not true. He *is* everywhere at once, and He does *not* need me. He wants me. He wants the relationship with me. And He set it up so that *I need Him*. But He does not need me.

Remember that in the tree of life, matters of good and evil are settled relationally. That works only if I trust the One with whom I am in relationship.

Look at this Do/Don't list again, and look at whether some of the things we think are bad, God would actually lead someone to do, in faith. You can easily see that God might say something is bad for one person but good for another. For instance, God might tell a shy person to speak up, but He might tell an outgoing person to be quiet. Right?

Granted, those are subjective leadings, so what about His hard and fast rules? His commandments? In Acts 10:9-16, God gives Peter a vision telling him he can eat non-kosher food. This man has been eating kosher *his whole life*, in obedience to God, and now God tells him that previously unclean food is now clean. This is so far outside of what Peter knows to please God that God has to give him the vision three times! Still, Peter resists. God has to say, "What God has cleansed, no longer consider unholy," before Peter will act on it.

> We think we know what is good and even what is biblical, but God surprises us.

We know that God certainly condemns harlotry. We are not to play the harlot with false idols, and we are not to play the harlot literally. Yet in Hosea 1:2, God tells Hosea: "Go, take to yourself a wife of harlotry and have children of harlotry; for the land commits flagrant harlotry, forsaking the LORD." He does this to paint a picture of Israel, who has been a harlot to God. But imagine being Hosea, living in the old covenant, and being told to take a harlot as your wife. It is unthinkable.

We cannot predict God. We think we know what is good and even what is biblical, but God surprises us. We must learn to hear His voice. It is about hearing God and following Him, even though we don't know what He's going to do. That's where the walk is. Faith comes in the unseen, not the seen (Hebrews 11:1). Once He explains it to us, we will do it (...sometimes!). But the test is doing it only because He says so. That's why Hebrews 11:6 says: "Without faith it is impossible to please Him."

This is a matter of life and death. Jesus brings life. But the list, or the law, brings death.

Let's look at those lists again. Take haunted houses. I think most of us would put haunted houses on the Don't list, wouldn't we? Last year, my friend's daughter wanted to go to a haunted house with her friends. Mom said, "No!" - for all the right reasons. But the mom prayed about it, and to her surprise, the Lord said, *Let her go.* Well, the girl went. The next day, she was supposed to go again, but she said to her mom, "I'm not going. It wasn't very good." (The Lord had been speaking to her as well.) Now, the girl has learned something about hearing the Lord, and that all things are lawful but not all things are profitable. That's something the Lord teaches us more effectively than any law (which only drives up desire, Romans 7:8). And Mom's faith was deepened. God is not as concerned about a haunted house as He is about our hearts. *He longs for our hearts.*

Around the same time, my son Chris went to a haunted house. I have never gone to them because I can't understand the attraction, and because I have struggled with so much fear - a haunted house is the last place I would want to go. Well, Chris really wanted me to go with him. I said, "No! Forget it!" But the Lord told me to go. I said, "You're kidding." Again He said, *Go,* and I said, "Okay." He'd been working on my fears for some time, so I thought His leading had to do with that. Now to hear Chris tell it, there were bruises in his arm from me squeezing it as we crept through this haunted house. But let me tell you something: I was not afraid. In fact, I enjoyed this special appointment God had provided for victory over this fear!

All of us would put haunted houses on the evil list. Yet, God used one to heal some deep fears in me, to accomplish His good and perfect will. This is what it is to eat from the tree of life, knowing the personal, intimate leading of the Lord. He uses what He wants to accomplish His purposes. And it's always amazing. I'm not saying to put haunted houses on the good list either. I'm saying, dispense with the lists, and listen to the Lord.

Now, let me guess what you're thinking: *How can I dispense with the lists? The kids'll do something horrible!* That was the belief of Jane and John Doe, the family with the perfect kids who went off the deep end. But, that is not true. They discovered that the ones who do something horrible are the ones who *have* lived under the lists and won't take it anymore. The ones who learn to eat from the tree of life instead of the tree of knowledge don't do the horrible things. I will share more stories with you as we go, but for now, I'll say this: what we think will happen when we throw away the to-do list is the opposite of what actually happens.

It took me some years to wrap my mind around this huge concept, but if you can do it, it will revolutionize your relationship with the Lord and with your kids.

Here's another real life example for you. My daughter Annie wanted us to read a certain book as a family. It was a book "banned" by the Christian community because of the content, and I was right in there with the best of them, saying, "No." But my daughter, very grounded in the Lord, asked me to pray about it. Praying is never the wrong thing to do, so I did. I could hear the Spirit whisper to me, *There is nothing wrong with this book.*

Then He gave me the verse about eating meat sacrificed to idols - 1 Corinthians 10: 23-33: "All things are lawful, but not all things are profitable. All things are lawful, but not all things edify. Let no one seek his own good, but that of his neighbor. Eat anything that is sold in the meat market without asking questions for conscience' sake; *for the earth is the Lord's and all it contains*. If one of the unbelievers invites you and you want to go, eat anything that is set before you without asking questions for conscience' sake. But if anyone says to you, "This is meat sacrificed to idols," do not eat it, for the sake of the one who informed you, and for conscience' sake; I mean not your own conscience, but the other man's; for why is my freedom judged by another's conscience? If I partake with thankfulness, why am I slandered concerning that for which I give thanks? Whether, then, you eat or drink or whatever you do, do all to the glory of God. Give no offense either to Jews or to Greeks or to the church of God; just as I also please all men in all things, not seeking my own profit but the profit of the many, so that they may be saved." (See 1 Corinthians 8:1-18; 1 Corinthians 10:23-33 for more about meat sacrificed to idols and how that relates to the law.)

> As Augustine said, "Love God with all your heart and do as you please."

Eating meat sacrificed to idols: is it sin or not? This was important because nearly all of the meat available in the marketplace at the time had been sacrificed to idols. The *only* way to make sense of the verse about idol meat is by our personal, intimate relationship with God, knowing He wants us listening to Him, no longer following the law. Remember, when you eat from the tree of knowledge, you settle good and evil *legalistically*. But when you eat from the tree of life, you settle good and evil *relationally*. The relationship is the difference between biblical Christianity and every other faith.

Now understand this point: I had in my hand a controversial book, banned by most Christians, and I prayed for God to tell me whether to read it with my children. My heart was to obey Him. He told me in His still small voice, through 1 Corinthians 8, that there was nothing wrong with this book. This was as profound to me as it was to Peter to be told to eat non-kosher meat, and to Hosea to marry a harlot. Life-altering. As Annie began to read the book aloud to all of us, I was praying, *Lord! If I misheard You, please tell me!* Peter must have felt this way when he bit into that first ham sandwich. But God *affirmed* it, and reading that book together became a wonderful family experience.

As Augustine said, "Love God with all your heart and do as you please." Do you see how much freedom this gives us? It's remarkable. Augustine was not disposed to pushing the limit as far as he could just short of trouble. His writings show that his heart longed to be worthy of the name of Christ - he followed Him with all his heart. But he had discovered something about God that perhaps few Christians actually discover; that is, the meaning of Galatians 5:1: "It was for freedom that Christ set us free." To turn our attention from deciding the good list and the evil list, and to focus instead on the Lord, is freeing indeed!

> They loved their children. But they couldn't let go of their lists.

Be clear, this is *not* the same as post-modern relativism, which says: "Whatever is true for you is fine and whatever is true for me is fine." Relativism is based on doing what is right in your own eyes - the description of sin throughout the Old Testament. I am talking about hearing and responding to the voice of the Lord. This personal relationship is the foundation of a dynamic Christian walk.

We owe it to our children to seek the Lord on their behalf and do what He guides us to do. These aren't cardboard cutouts that we're raising where we pick out this clothing style, that college, this career, that mate. These are real people with real wills and opinions and relationships with the Lord. Jesus never treated people like cardboard cutouts. We owe it to the health of our relationships to listen to Him regarding each child and each situation.

John and Jane Doe had a vision of how they wanted their kids to turn out. They interacted with that vision rather than with the real children sitting around the table. They loved their children. But they couldn't let go of their lists.

Following the Lord is not a trick, a sneaky way to do what you want. On the contrary, it requires much more submission than it does to keep the lists. A friend read this chapter for me, and she said: "That's fine for you because you are a mature believer. But I'm worried about the new believer who will take it as freedom to do what they want." But the truth is, we do have freedom. God gives us that freedom when He gives us our free will. If He didn't value freedom, He never would have allowed the fall and all that has come from it. Living and growing in the Lord is how we become a mature believer. No one becomes mature without mistakes along the way. No one becomes mature without the Lord's personal growth and guidance. I shudder to look back on some idiotic things I've said and done. Don't you? Remember, it is all about the heart. The heart that longs to know Him has the freedom to pour a jar of expensive oil on Jesus' feet (John 12:3). Mary did not reason her way to that decision, but was driven by love for her Savior. May we be so driven.

Heartwork

1. Think of something the Lord has led you to do that didn't fit your ideas. How has He led you that was not on the Do list.
2. Did you do it? How did it turn out?
3. Do you know any families whose children have rebelled? Ask the Lord to show you what He wants you to see about them.
4. Ask the Lord what items you have on your Do/Don't list. Ask Him how He would lead you with it.
5. Ask your teens if there's anything they feel bound to do "be cause that's what we do."
6. Ask if they would like to revisit those items with you.

• • •

chapter 4
THEY'RE GOING TO LOOK LIKE YOU

> *"Two boys grew up to speak of their parents' influence. Both boys recalled how their parents treated them as children. The first said, 'Once you know your family loves you, you are free to try anything. You are free to fail and free to succeed.' The second recorded a deep hatred of his cruel and abusive father. What you do today as parents can literally shape tomorrow's world. By the way - the two boys? The first... President George W. Bush. The other? Adolf Hitler."* Mark Merrill, Family Minute

> *"The apple doesn't fall far from the tree."* Unknown

She's Got Your Nose!

Children look like their parents. They may be anything from a spitting image to having only a vague resemblance, but the traces are there. I saw a very cute girl at the orthodontist, with a style of hair and clothing that were her own. She had an adorable, animated personality, and I noticed she didn't have much of a chin. Then I saw her dad! I knew it was her dad - he had no chin. As cute as she made herself, there was no escaping that family trait. We can put time and distance between us and our parents - throwing in our own clothes and style and ideas - but there's that chin to give it away! My daughter Annie looks just like my husband - but she has my mother's mouth. Isn't that strange? How does God do that?

And who hasn't looked in the mirror and shrieked: "I look like my mother!"

This is true with character also. One of my children, I found, has an irritating habit of demanding that everything be fair - that is, in her favor! If she couldn't hit the ball back, then it was out of bounds. Or if she couldn't return the serve, it was too low. I was watching her one day, quite irritated by this, and the Lord suddenly reminded me that I did the same thing at that age! *How in the world did I convey that to her?* I haven't done that since I was young, and we have some thirty years between us! Is it genetic? Or in some way, have I communicated that same need to be right... because clearly that is my imprint.

> "They have bad attitudes.' Debi responded, 'No, it's you that has the bad attitude.'"

My dear friend learned not to cry growing up because her father would spank her for it. When her young son's goldfish died, he fought back tears, saying, "Mommy, I'm trying not to cry!" Her heart broke. She never meant to convey that it was not okay to cry, but she did.

Our attitudes impact those around us more than we realize. Listen to this excerpt from an article by Debi Pearl about parenting: "A mother complained to me... 'The children frustrate me so much. They are always irritating one another... They are always complaining and whining about something. I get frustrated and spank them, but it does no good.' Debi interrupted, 'Yes, it is an attitude problem.' The weary mother hastily agreed, 'That's it! They have bad attitudes.' Debi responded, 'No, it's you that has the bad attitude.' Are you a frustrated parent? If parenting is not enjoyable, be assured, you have a bad attitude. When your children look into your face, what do they see? They are not fooled. They know what you feel about them."

This article hit me so hard I remember it many years later. I know how frustrated we get when things are difficult or aren't turning out as we had hoped. It's hard to see, and harder to admit, that some of those things that irritate us about our children originated in us.

My point is *not* to blame ourselves. We probably got it from our parents, who got it from their parents... I have bestowed many traits on my children that I would rather neither of us had, but there it is. As we become aware of this is, we know where to look to begin to fix it.

We can try to change our kids, but they are going to turn out something like us (or have strains of us). That similarity seems as random and uncontrollable as our physical resemblance.

Sometimes we just want to give up! Really, the job is simply too big, too overwhelming, too unpredictable. *But*... as we have already seen, we have one option as parents: to press into the Lord. And that has always been our only option.

He Learns by Watching You

It is said that as much as a child needs to know that his parents love him, he is far more secure knowing his parents love *each other*. I think we understand instinctively how true that is.

Here is a parallel. As much as your child needs you to teach him dependence on the Lord, he needs to see *your* dependence on the Lord. Teaching him may reach his head - and even change his actions - but not necessarily change his heart. But when he sees

> I have seen my reflection in my children so many times, that now if something is going on in the family, some dynamic, the first place I look is in the mirror.

you working through your struggles and depending on God to meet you there - for example, when he overhears you talking to the Lord while you're doing the dishes - you are showing him that God has real answers for real problems.

Our job as parents is to heed Matthew 6:33: "But seek first

His kingdom and His righteousness, and all these things will be added to you." He will meet all our needs.

C.S. Lewis says: "Put first things first, and you will have first things with second things thrown in. But put second things first and you will lose both first and second things."

I have seen my reflection in my children so many times, that now if something is going on in the family, some dynamic, the first place I look is in the mirror. Ask Him how you (or your spouse) figure into this. Press into Him. This is humbling, because I'd really rather correct *my children* than find a weakness in me. But look at the bright side - if I can correct something in me, then I have essentially corrected it in them!

I don't mean that every time brother hauls off and whacks sister, you pause for introspection. I am saying that when you see a recurring pattern, it's time to ask the Lord where that pattern began, and for His solution.

As I was discipling a dear friend, the Lord had just revealed how afraid she is to speak up for what she wants and needs. She is debilitated in her ability to say something difficult to her husband. Her son was over to play with my son, and I noticed that he had a very tough time telling me what he needed or wanted. Did he want a sandwich or hot dog for lunch? He didn't care. Mustard or mayo? Doesn't matter. It hit me how much he is like his mother! I mentioned it to her, because we had just been talking about this very thing. She said, "How do I get him to express himself?" I said, "*You* have to express yourself!" He will only learn it by seeing it modeled. It turned out to be the very area God was working on in her.

If we want to find something, we have to look for it in the right place. It's like the boy who looked for his coin under the lamppost because "the light is better there." The light may be better there, but if it's not where you lost it, it won't be where you find it. We can look all we want for the origin of a certain flesh pattern in our kids. But it may be in us.

Remember: we do not need to condemn ourselves. "There is

therefore now no condemnation for those who are in Christ Jesus" (Romans 8:1). But if we want healing, we have to look in the right spot.

There is a fine balance between taking too much or too little responsibility for problems with our children. Some mothers are prone to blaming themselves. If this sounds like you, you need to let the Lord show us where your child is in error. To excuse your children because you are an imperfect parent, or to wait until you become perfect to train them, does no good at all. All of us are imperfect, and we must still do our best to train our children.

On the other hand, many of us need to humble ourselves enough to let God reveal a great log in our own eye (Matthew 7:3). In any kind of effective counseling, both parties must look at their part in the breakdown. Though one person may bear much more responsibility than the other, a breakdown is almost never completely one person's fault. Some friends of ours gave their testimony about the husband's affair, and *both* of them took responsibility for their part. Yes, of course he was at fault. He made an awful mistake. He was absolutely wrong. But she admits having rejected him in many ways. That does not relieve his responsibility, but gives her a place to look as well. Do you see what I mean? This kind of thing cannot be foisted upon someone, but each person in a problem needs to seek the Lord about his own responsibility.

On the one hand, our children's actions are their own, they are responsible, and they will have their own consequences. On the other hand, the apple doesn't fall far from the tree, and we end up acting just like our parents! So, ask the Lord to guide you and show you that balance. It is a mystery. But it is not too hard for God.

Refiner's Fire

This impact on your kids is high motivation to let God work in you. And He will work in you, in the refiner's fire. You may have heard how a silversmith refines silver. He heats it up until all the impurities float to the surface. Then he sloughs them off. How does he know when all the impurities come out? When he can see himself in the silver! Equally important is that the silversmith does not heat the silver one moment longer than necessary because that would ruin the silver.

And so our heavenly Father does not allow one more moment of pain than we need for refinement. God's process of removing our impurities can be long and painful indeed. But when the pain has done its work, it will be lifted. And in the end, we will reflect Him.

The Sunny Side

This also means you can train your children by doing what you want them to do, *over time*. I have been overwhelmed by the thought of modeling behavior for my children, because I didn't think I had it in me, to be what I wanted them to be. I was too selfish and short-tempered and disorganized. How could I model the opposite? But when I turned my attention to Him, growing in Him, it's amazing how much they picked up from me. Because they do as I do, changes in me became changes in them. Who knew how much power there is in simply surrendering to Him, in good faith, and letting Him cause the increase?

You think they're not paying attention? *Believe me*, they are.

The point of this whole chapter is to realize that as parents, we need to do our own submitting to the Lord, even as we to entreat our children to submit. We will talk plenty more about what God does in the parent's half of the parent-child relationship. Meanwhile, the next section will help us disentangle the parent's walk from the child's.

Heartwork

1. What traits in you trace back to your parents?
2. What traits in your children trace back to you or your

spouse?
3. Thank God for those traits in you and your child.
4. Ask God to show you the areas He is working in your child, including progress already made. Is there anything you need to do, to nurture that growth?
5. What traits is He working in you, including progress already made?
6. Please ask the Lord to remove any guilt you feel from unwittingly passing on your humanness to your kids. And ask Him to comfort you in the job you've done so far - to nurture you and encourage you.
7. Where are you dependent on the Lord?
8. Where are you independent? Are you willing to surrender those areas?
9. Ask the Lord what else He would show you now.

• • •

41

chapter 5
OUT OF CONTROL

> "The prestige of government has undoubtedly been lowered considerably by the prohibition law. For nothing is more destructive of respect for the government and the law of the land than passing laws which cannot be enforced. It is an open secret that the dangerous increase of crime in the United States is closely connected with this." Albert Einstein

> "I would rather be exposed to the inconveniences attending too much liberty than to those attening too small a degree of it." Thomas Jefferson

> "Rules without relationship equals rebellion" Unknown

> "Why do the strictest families always lose their first-born?" Beth, a mom, observing legalistic parenting

Our money belongs not to us but to God, and is only on loan to us to steward for a while. It seems like it's ours, but it's not. The same is true with our children. They seem like they're ours, but they're not. As people with wills of their own, kids are even less ours than our money.

Good Christian stewards have lost their fortunes through no fault of their own. So have good Christian parents lost their children through no fault of their own (children who rebel or walk away from the faith). God is sovereign over our finances, even when it doesn't look like it, and God is sovereign over our children, even when it doesn't look like it. We are not God, and He has given us limited authority over our children. (We can't do whatever we want to them, right?)

The more we submit our financial decisions to God, the better our finances work out. And the more we submit our authority to Him (the more we seek His input on how to guide our children), the more we will like the result!

God is your teen's creator, guide, protector, sovereign authority and Savior. Your job is to entrust them to Him.

The biggest temptation for Christian parents is not to let their children separate early enough or fully enough, to make their own choices and take the consequences for them. Let's face it - it's scary out there! But take heart – the very voice of the creator of the universe speaks personally and lovingly to us about our teens. And He loves them.

A Case Study

When Rehoboam became king (I Kings 12), the people petitioned him to lighten the heavy burden his father Solomon had put on them. King Rehoboam sought counsel from the wise old men who had served Solomon faithfully; they said: "'If you will be a servant to this people today, and will serve them and grant them their petition, and speak good words to them, then they will be your servants forever' (v. 7).

"But he forsook the counsel of the elders... and consulted with the young men who grew up with him and served him. And they said: 'Thus you shall say to this people who spoke to you, saying, 'Your father made our yoke heavy, now you make it lighter for us!' But you shall speak to them, 'My little finger is thicker than my father's loins!... Whereas my father loaded you with a heavy yoke, I will add to your yoke; my father disciplined you with whips, but I will discipline you with scorpions (v. 10).'"

King Rehoboam considered for three days, then he answered the people harshly. "For he *forsook the advice of the elders which they had given him, and he spoke to them according to the advice of the young men*, saying, 'My father made your yoke heavy, but I will add to your yoke; my father disciplined you with whips, but I will discipline you with scorpions.' So the king did not listen to the people; for it was a turn of events from the LORD, that He might establish His word… (v. 13-15)."

The result of the king's decision is summed up in verse 19: "So Israel has been in rebellion against the house of David to this day."

What a tragic story. Rehoboam received, from experienced elders, counsel that would make the people love him. But in his pride, he rejected their wisdom, thinking his power was unlimited. And the people rebelled. Indeed, rules without relationship equals rebellion.

> Nurturing human beings into adulthood must be done in God's power, not ours.

My heart weeps for parents who think their power is unlimited and put burdens on their children that "provoke them to wrath." It results in tragedy, and the parents wonder what happened.

My father put enormous burdens on my brother Pete. Pete couldn't take it anymore and rebelled. One thing led to another, Pete joined a gang and he was murdered at age seventeen. An unnecessary tragedy. You cannot keep turning up the heat on someone and not expect him to boil over.

Nurturing human beings into adulthood must be done in God's power, not ours. That requires little control and a lot of submission.

Here is the bold truth about controllers: they produce exactly what they fear producing. One mom so valued her daughters' virtue that she did everything *in her power* to keep them pure. Ironically, the high-control path she took drove them straight into the thing she dreaded most: rebellious promiscuity.

My friend Beth and I were observing the many strict, legalistic families whose kids had fallen away, especially the oldest (who often gets the brunt of the strictness). Beth astutely asked: "Why do the strictest families always lose their firstborn?" It is a question worth asking.

We've heard the verse: "Children obey your parents in the Lord, for this is right," (Ephesians 6:1). But I am fascinated to think what comes only three verses later: "Fathers, do not provoke your children to anger, but bring them up in the discipline and instruction of the Lord," or "the nurture and admonition of the Lord." I have heard controlling fathers quote: "Children obey your parents." But I have never heard any of them quote, "Fathers, do not provoke your children to anger." Isn't that curious? You would think they don't know it…

Forever quoting only the first verse is a gross distortion.

I'm going to say something very bold here: If you will not bow to God regarding His direction for you as a parent, you stand to lose your child. I've seen it happen in half a dozen families.

But instead of talking about them, let me tell you what happened with my own son. First, understand that my father was extremely hard on us, piling on impossible expectations, especially with the boys. Perhaps he wanted to realize his dreams through them, to make his life count. He called them stupid and said they were going to fail life. It wreaked unbelievable damage on the boys, three of whom died young. My father did not know God, and he certainly did not understand trusting Him. Controllers do not understand trusting God – or they would give up control. And I carried my father's predisposition against boys into our family, to our sons.

So, here I am with Chris at age fourteen, and I'm thinking we have a good relationship. I know there were issues in our family, but it's generally good. Well, Rob and I are about to go out to dinner, and I'm cleaning up, waiting for him to come out so we can go. After a while, I'm thinking, *where is he?* After an hour, he comes out of our room with Chris, and something is definitely up.

I say, "What's going on?" He just leads me out the door.

In the car, he proceeds to tell me how Chris has been crying for an hour, telling him that no matter what he does, *I* am not satisfied. For example, he will clean the kitchen, and I'll say, "You didn't sweep the floor." I never encourage him; I don't embrace him for who he is.

This came as a devastating blow to me, as you can imagine. Me, with the gift of encouragement. But my son did not know that. I had no idea this was a problem in our relationship, but I knew as Rob said it, it was true. I was in tears by now, of course. We got to the restaurant and found a private booth, where I sat crying, asking God to help me through this horrible time.

Rob helped me see where I could make changes. He is really good with our kids, and he knew where I was missing the mark. But this was a generational problem, a spiritual battle that I needed God to heal. I had become my father. *Oh, God help me!* I never viewed myself as being like my father – even though I had his temper. But now I saw that I had his attitude toward my boys – and I was losing them. I did not delight in Chris, even though he was delightful. So I prayed that God would delight in him through me. I prayed that God would show me how *He* sees Chris. It is my job to delight in him. I love this boy. The baby I always wanted – smart, adorable, funny – he's an outstanding son. And that's not even the point. He's my *son*! I never meant to reject him through impossible standards.

Over a period of months – which is quick – God healed my heart toward him. I did come to delight in him. We're very close now. On my last Mother's Day card he wrote this: *Every time you say you're proud of me, inside I know I wouldn't be anything if it weren't for you. I can't say how much I admire you as a mother. Love, Christopher.*

This was a gift from God! All I did was surrender to God's leading. Without His power, my son would have fallen away like so many others. I had started down a road that was going to destroy our relationship and produce a wounded, broken adult.

Counselors spend hour after hour with wounded people – in wounded marriages, raising wounded children – men and women who have been wounded by parents unwilling to bend to God's breaking. Yes, God is able to heal those wounded people, as He uses their pain to drive them into dependence on Him. He works that way. But I want my son. If I had not surrendered, I would have lost him. Instead, I surrendered my heart and humbled myself (and believe me, it was humbling), and God restored us.

Counselors also see people whose parents did not express their love for them, nor convey how much God loves them. Parents love their children. But they often do not express their love as their kids need to hear it.

We may not have received what we needed from our parents, but this is the good news of God's restoration: He will provide.

> …fathers who abuse and control and push their children to a goal may well achieve it *in their own power*. But it will be a sick and dead thing.

A couple of years ago, a family came to me for counseling, seeking resolution after their son, "Jake," attempted suicide. Jake had already told me he did not feel loved or accepted by his father. I counseled the parents to embrace their son, express their unconditional love for him, and allow him to make some decisions for himself – like spending time with his older brother who loved him so much. (I only knew this because God had shown it to me, played out in various lives.) While the mother was in agreement, the father was not. Later, the parents met with a different counselor, who told them to kick the son out. They chose that counsel. Now, three years later, Jake is long gone, the the mother laments having lost all contact with him, and the father has not humbled himself. It is Rehoboam all over again, choosing the counsel that allowed him prideful, high control, but ended in tragedy.

It takes courage to ask the Lord whether you or your spouse

is controlling. It takes more courage to ask your teen. It takes the most courage for the teen to say yes. Let God show you whether you are communicating unconditional, fully granted love to your children. If these issues exist, nothing provides more family healing than to humble yourself to His healing.

If there *are* issues, ask for help. Ask God where to go for the help you need. There is no shame in needing help. The shame is in stiffening your neck to God and refusing the help He wants to give you.

Control Out of Control

Michael Jackson was an immensely talented child prodigy. He could sing, dance, create and perform like no one else. But reports allege that his father was an abusive controller who worked hard to make his children stars. He did it! He brought them fame beyond their wildest dreams! But he ended up with a son whose superstar fame has been eclipsed by personal scandal and tragedy. The point is crystal clear: fathers who abuse and control and push their children to a goal may well achieve it in their own power. But it will be a sick and dead thing.

God gave us *all* unique, wonderful children. When He endowed our precious children with all their great potential, He never intended for *us* to make it happen. God gives us opportunity to facilitate our children's dreams as *He* leads us; we cannot become God no matter how hard we try. Even if we succeed beyond our wildest dreams in achieving success for our children, if we are not submitted to God, we missed it.

We control our children when we have unreachable expectations or offer conditional acceptance. We think this will inspire them to do better. But unreachable expectations do *not* inspire anyone to greatness. No one drew near to the heart of God by keeping the law. And no one drew near to the heart of their parents by meeting their standards. The law drives us to defeat. After all, that is the purpose of the law (Galatians 3:24-25).

"Monica's" father was a legalistic, controlling abuser. Monica looked so forward to turning eighteen, hoping finally to gain some freedom that she had so long desired – we're talking freedom to go to the mall or to a friend's house. At the breakfast table she said, "I can't wait to turn eighteen! I'll finally be an adult." You know what her father said? "Monica, nothing will change when you turn eighteen." Can you just feel the heart being sucked right out of her?

Things *did* change, because she left home at eighteen – against Dad's wishes. The Lord called her out, showing her that she needed to be out of her father's deathgrip. It was a major crack in the family structure. More cracks followed. The second daughter was removed by Children's Protective Services (which takes a lot of abuse to accomplish). The third daughter is cutting.

Make no mistake: if parents won't surrender to God's control, He will wrest control away. You may have seen people who would not give control of their money to God, and He pulled it from them. It is the same with our kids. It is not punishment; it is removing our idols so we can see Him. How much better to give up control to the One who has ultimate right to control, than to have it torn away because we wouldn't bow to Him.

Here's the thing: this father had had many warnings – from close friends, from extended family, from church leaders, and from his children. But he was not willing to listen.

As for Monica… she has sought the Lord, she has prayed and listened to His voice. And God has revealed Himself as her Daddy in tender ways, providing direction and encouragement. She has as close a relationship with God as anybody could ever want for their daughter – which is remarkable, given the picture of God her father painted. But her father, who has still not humbled himself, is missing it all. His pride was more indispensable to him than his daughter, and rather than lose his pride, he lost her.

Contrast that to a dear friend whose daughter got a scholarship to her choice university. The only trouble was that it was across the country! My friend started to panic, worried about her daughter's purity, because she would be so far away. The girl was already committed to purity, but mom was worried that she might not be able to stick with it. So she asked me what I thought about her making a contract with her daughter. I said, "Does your daughter want a contract?"

She said, "Well, it was my idea."

"Oh. What do you think it will accomplish? And will be you be there to enforce it?"

"No!" she said. She started to see that this was only something to make her feel better. It had no real power. My friend already had what she wanted – a girl who was completely committed to purity. A contract was *not* going to strengthen her commitment. But it *would* reveal how powerless the mother is to hold her daugh-

> Control. You want to kick it like a bad habit.

ter to purity. She tells me now that everything has been great, the girl is doing so well – without a contract – and she realizes that the idea was motivated by fear, not by the Lord. God was the only One to whom she could entrust her daughter's purity all along.

Don't Raise Co-Dependents

By training our children to depend on the Lord, we prepare them to unfold into the good plans the Lord has for them, plans for a future and hope, rather than setting them up to seek approval, which makes them co-dependent. They need our encouragement and we are called to provide it lavishly (more on that in chapter twelve). But we are not designed to sustain nor be sustained by the granting or withholding of approval. We cannot provide enough praise to sustain another person, and another's praise will not sustain us. When we teach our children that they are complete in the Lord (instead of training them to need our approval), we set them up for healthy adult relationships.

Control. You want to kick it like a bad habit. We think it is the way to get what we want, but ultimately, it kills what we love. Those you hold onto with control will either squirm away from you or die in your hand. It is not God's way. You could not have predicted your own path to the Lord, and you can't predict your teen's. When I was a teenager, we would go down the rapids in innertubes. One time, I lost my tube, which is dangerous because of hidden rocks. I couldn't stop myself, so I pulled my legs up and rode with the current until I could get out. Sometimes our children seem to be going down a river with no tube and we don't even know where the rocks are until our kids bash into them. But God knows every rock, every danger, and He knows how to protect our kids. He knows just what to allow and what to prevent. God is their tube.

This is a tough concept. Actually, the concept is not tough; the doing it is tough. But understand – high control fractures a family. God, who has every right to control us, does not; He gives us freedom (Galatians 5:1). Even our very eternity is in our hands (John 3:16). If you haven't already seen this, you will: your family will thrive when you stop controlling them.

Unfortunately, this situation is often like the father in the movie, Dead Poet's Society: his overbearing control is visible to everyone but him. And when things go terribly wrong, he blames everyone but himself. Many parents go that route, and they pay a high price, as do their children.

If the Lord is speaking to you, please, surrender. Pull up your legs and let the Lord take you down these rapids. It is scary, but He will bring you through it like you cannot imagine.

Heartwork

1. Ask God to show you if you are at all like Rehoboam.
2. Seek the Lord whole-heartedly about whether you are controlling.
3. Ask Him if your spouse is controlling.
4. If you are willing, ask your teen whether you or your spouse

is controlling. But you will have to grant freedom to speak without repercussion. (The more controlling the parent, the more the teen is at risk in telling them so.)

5. Ask Him to guide you in any area He has revealed to you.
6. Ask God if you are trying to achieve for your children. What goals is He asking you to surrender?
7. What choices is God asking you to let your teen make?
8. Ask God what else He would like to show you now, including steps to take.

• • •

whose journey is it?

chapter 6
SCOPE AND SEQUENCE

> *"We don't break God's rules; we break ourselves over God's rules."* Unknown

> *"We want to keep our kids from the very things that brought us to the Lord."* Mike Wells

> *"Oh, we're gonna hurt him! We'll just try to hurt him as little as possible."* Chris' Oral Surgeon

Surrendering increasing amounts of control to God can be a challenge for the best of parents. Sometimes it's hard to see the long-range vision God has for our kids and harder to see how their crisis du jour will turn into maturity sufficient to handle life on their own.

Let me try to ease your mind, by reminding us how completely God has our kids' lives mapped out. "'For I know the plans that I have for you,' declares the Lord, 'plans for welfare and not calamity to give you a future and a hope'" (Jeremiah 29:11). He has their scope and sequence lined out for them – just like when we were in school and we had a certain course of study to cover (scope) and in a certain order (sequence). At the time, the various particulars – maybe sine and cosine – seemed random, even unnecessary. But it actually fit into an overall course of study.

God also has the scope and sequence. He knows what elements they need, when they need it, and how to teach them most effectively. It appears random to us; it appears that somehow our child is just

> God continually gives us way more than we can handle – because He doesn't want us handling it; He wants us to let Him handle it.

being a pain, or our spouse is being a pain, or life is being a pain. But He has got a scope and sequence mapped out for our child's walk, our spouse's walk, and our walk. Our job is to surrender to *His* scope and sequence. We can't even begin to plan what they need to grow deeply and completely in the Lord.

You have heard that God won't give you more than you can handle. But that is nowhere in the Bible, and it is not true. God continually gives us way more than we can handle – because He doesn't want us handling it; He wants us to let Him handle it.

The Bible *does* say: "No temptation has overtaken you but such as is common to man; and God is faithful, *who will not allow you to be tempted beyond what you are able*, but with the temptation will provide the way of escape also, so that you will be able to endure it" (1 Corinthians 10:13, emphasis added). He is telling us that He will not drive us over the edge with impossible situations but will provide a way of escape from temptation. He is *always* there for us.

But that is not the same as saying that He is going to give us the easy way out.

Here's the interesting thing: we pray for God's mercy, patience, grace – but where do those things show up? In times that require them.

If I want God's patience, I will see it by being driven to the edge of my own patience and realizing I can only have more if I use His. If I want to know God's grace, I won't find it in a small situation that my grace will cover, but in a big situation where I must have His grace or I won't have any.

You see, God does not keep us in situations that fit within our abilities, because honing our abilities is not the goal. God does not want us to use our abilities but to surrender to His abilities. God does not want us handling our situations; on the contrary, He allows us to get to the end of ourselves until we see that we need Him to handle things for us. Increased dependence on Him is the goal.

Even Jesus submitted his every action to God, and God carried Him. That is our assignment as well.

My son Chris had four wisdom teeth removed. Two of them were sideways, so they couldn't just pull them, they had to break them and then take them out in pieces. Just before the surgery I said to the doctor, "Don't hurt him!"

The doctor said, "Oh, we're gonna hurt him. We'll just try to hurt him as little as possible." Isn't that funny?

> We say, "Lord, help our kids know You, love You, trust You, put You first." But then we don't want Him to do any of the things that accomplish that!

That is a perfect picture of how this brokenness works with God. He has to hurt us (or allow us to be hurt, if you prefer). Pain is an unavoidable part of the process. But He hurts us as little as possible, and He gets us to the other side better and more whole than before.

Those winding paths that brought us to a deeper understanding of the Lord? Those things we wish we hadn't had to go through? Our big mistakes? Those are the very things that God used to bring us to a deeper understanding of Him. We must allow God to use those same methods on our teens. We say, "Lord, help our kids know You, love You, trust You, put You first." But then we don't want Him to do any of the things that accomplish that! Do you remember being seventeen? Being nineteen? Being an idiot? I certainly do! We were all there. If you can't remember it, because you walked the straight and narrow – bless you! But ask the Lord what means He has used to deepen your faith. (If you cannot recall circumstances that deepened your faith, you might want to buckle your seatbelt.) But I believe that if you ask Him, He'll remind you of times He was breaking you, times when you struggled and questioned and wanted out.

God wants us to surrender the "title deed" of our children's faith from us to Him. That's what the eighteen years is about. We were put in custody of them only temporarily to give them a picture of the God they will surrender to for the rest of their lives. (Amazing God chose us to do that, isn't it? I mean, just *look* at us!) We were always only temporary custodians, a picture of Him; He always intended to establish direct authority over them. The more we understand God's goal and surrender to it, the easier it is for everyone.

Please hear this: God wants direct access to our children. As He pulls control from us, the less we struggle against it, the easier that transition becomes. When we fight against it, we *and our children* suffer. Like a job when it's time to move on, the more we resist, the more embarrassing it becomes – especially if the police have to escort us off the premises. Better to go when the time is right and let God be God.

The best part is that God is completely trustworthy. That's really what it comes down to. If we won't surrender our teens to Him, it is usually an issue of fear for them and a lack of trust in Him. If that is so, the issue is between us and Him. It has nothing to do with our children.

Remember, He knows how to break them. If their path of brokenness were up to us, we wouldn't know where to begin.

Isaiah 46: 9-10 says: "…I am God, and there is no other; I am God, and there is none like Me, Declaring the end from the beginning, And from ancient times things that are not yet done, Saying, 'My counsel shall stand, And I will do all My pleasure.'"

That is, at the very beginning, He knows what the end is. We don't. We have to come up with knowledge we don't have. He is the only One who can map out our course because He's already seen the end of it.

We already talked about which tree to eat from, but let me

tell you that it is very difficult to move away from the Tree of the Knowledge of Good and Evil (after a lifetime of eating from it), when we're faced with something we'd consider a bad situation. Think for a minute about Mary coming home from her visit with her cousin Elizabeth (Luke 1). Can you imagine Mary's parents' response? *Uh, hello!* Just like if your daughter got pregnant. Is that about one of the worst things you could imagine? Not the worst, but we would definitely say, "This is on my bad list." Absolutely. Now I'm going to tell you a little story.

My mother had a tragic childhood, losing her mother at seven, then living in foster homes. When her father remarried, my mother was able to live at home again (that's how they did it in those days). Meanwhile, she had suffered much abuse. Not surprisingly, at sixteen, she got pregnant. I imagine that this moral, upright family in the 1940s was upset to find their daughter pregnant, although they embraced her and loved her through it. Abortions were not an option then, and I don't think my mother would have had one anyway. So she had my sister Karin. About four years later she married my dad and had six more children. Our family was complete bedlam, violence, and true danger.

Do you know who God used to save us, to protect all of us children from much harm and physical death? Karin. Do you know who eventually led us all to the Lord? Karin. Without her, none of us would have made it - I firmly believe that. But who could have known all that when my mother got pregnant at only sixteen? You see, we don't know the end from the beginning. And what looks tragic to us, what would definitely be on our bad list, God uses and allows and maybe even plans, to develop our relationship with Him. Neither of my parents knew the Lord. I believe that without Karin, we kids may never have known Him either. We are not God. And we look at things we didn't plan on and didn't expect and we say, "That's bad!" But we don't know that. They are part of the fabric of God weaving things together in our lives.

We often hear Romans 8:28 – the verse people always quote

when things "go wrong" – but we seldom include the next verse, v. 29, with it. "And we know that God causes all things to work together for good to those who love God, to those who are the called according to His purpose. For those whom He foreknew, He also predestined to become conformed to the image of His Son." For years I had no idea those verses went together! Those things God is working together for our good? The next verse tells us it is *for the purpose of conforming us to His image*. Oh wow! That changes everything! What a relief – if all those things that we don't like in our teens' lives (or in our lives) are for the purpose of conforming them (us) to His image! We can't want more than that!

> God uses satan to conform us and our children to His image.

Then two verses later, verse 31, says: "What then shall we say to these things? If God is for us, who is against us?" That tells me that even the enemy, the one we ultimately fear the most, can do nothing to me without God's permission. We don't need to be afraid of him. God knows what He's doing. In fact, if you think of the classic story of suffering in the Bible, Job, you notice something incredible. In Job 2:3, satan is wandering around on the earth, and God says to him, "Have you considered my servant Job?" God is the *author* of that trouble. It really proves that God has our scope and sequence planned out; the enemy thinks he's wreaking havoc, but he is no match for God. On the contrary, God uses satan to conform us and our children to His image.

If we start looking at our loved ones' lives from that perspective, we will begin to see challenges *not* as an interruption to their lives, but as His conforming us to His image.

Trusting God

I could tell you any number of stories to illustrate that we don't know the end from the beginning but God does. I will let one story represent our struggle against letting God have His way with our children.

Years ago, our friend's daughter was desperate to go to the private Christian college that her closest friends were going to. She pleaded with her father to send her, which only broke his heart, because in his wildest dreams he could not afford it. Had he the power, he would have moved heaven and earth to provide the desire of his daughter's heart. As it was, she reluctantly attended a local state college for which his company provided full scholarship.

Now, these many years later, she sees how mismatched her preferred college would have been for her, and how God equipped her specifically through the college He provided. She had no way to predict the many things He was going to do in her, through His selected provision.

Mature believers understand God's absolute ability to choose the best for us, even if we sometimes have trouble surrendering to Him. But as parents, submitting our children to Him can be especially tough. Our innate desire to provide as a parent often eclipses our trust in God's absolute ability to choose the *best* for them.

My husband's mother loved him and did whatever she could for him. She bailed him out of many youthful troubles. So, he never really felt the consequences of his choices – until they were too big for her to remove. He spent much of his thirties learning at God's hand, what he could have learned in his teens. She certainly meant well. But she unwittingly interfered with God's scope and sequence for him.

I say this as encouragement! We can default to trusting God! The less expensive state school is not second best – I know that because it is what God provided. He could certainly provide a way for the Christian college if that is what He wanted. And if that plan *we* know would be best for them would really be best, He would make it happen. He is God, after all. But He is the one with their scope and sequence, not us. If you persist in doing what seems best to you (as Gameliel said), "…you may even be found fighting against God" (Acts 5:39).

Our challenge, dear parent, especially with our children, is to trust Him as their Provider rather than doing whatever we can to make something happen that God may not want to happen.

In other cases, our children's hearts are not ready to receive what is best for them, and we cannot make it so. One couple struggled watching their daughter get involved with a destructive boyfriend, get hooked on drugs and then get pregnant. They sought rehab for her, but she would not go. This was not how they imagined life as they approached their 50s. They did everything possible, but they could not compel their daughter toward wisdom. I tell this story with compassion and sorrow for the soul that would foolishly choose what is right in her own eyes rather than the wisdom of the Lord. It may be as hard to watch as it is to go through – maybe harder. We try everything possible. I seek all possible solutions and do my best to implement them. My battlecry is: *Surely there is something we can do here!* But the heart-rending lesson is this: God will not compel people to choose what is best for them. (How much less can we compel them?) He will wait patiently as they exhaust their own methods, always ready to embrace them when they have finally come to the end of themselves. Then they will understand what they did not understand before: they do not have what it takes to be their own boss. He does.

How much more fitting that we, who know so much less, should likewise allow them to exhaust their own resources.

Dennis McCallum and Gary Delashmutt were two intellectual, atheist, hippies in the 60s. By God's amazing hand, they came to Christ and then started a small home church. Now they are the senior pastors of a large church where hundreds of people come to Christ every year.

Dennis tells about the time the police caught him using drugs - and it saved his life. We don't know what God has got planned. The key is to trust God wholeheartedly and to listen for His still, small voice.

A while back, I was talking to my Annie (who hardly makes a false step), about how God breaks us, breaking anything we would put before Him or put before knowing Him. She said, "Is it necessary to go through that pain if I'm not putting anything ahead of Him?" I know that if she could follow Him without the hard break, she would do that.

I said, "I don't know – Jesus said we will have trouble. But I do think the more we are listening, the easier it will be."

Now, a couple of things about this. First, the tender heart that wants to follow the Lord – it does not get any better than that. We cannot make anyone desire to hear Jesus any more than we can make someone accept Him as their Savior. But we want to look for it and nurture it.

The other thing is that hearing the Lord does not assure that life will not have trouble. Ask Job. He had no "secret sin" as God told his well-meaning friends (Job 42:8). When man sinned, he brought down all of creation with him. The earth groans under the weight of the sin, and we cannot "perform" to sidestep the effects of the fall. But we can turn our face to the Lord and let Him save us through it.

So when Annie was in Bible college, doing everything she was supposed to do, God did break her, showing her a subtle heart issue. I mean, it's the kind of breaking you want – it didn't involve drugs or pregnancy or police. It was all direct heart work. But as benign as it was, it was still *hard*. Rob longed to help her out of this, as he prayed for her. You know what God told him? *Let her struggle.* That's tough! Rob likes to make sure none of our family is suffering. He said, "It's like watching your child on a feeding tube." Letting God work in you is the challenge – especially when we're talking about your children. But God always has the redemptive plan.

You've heard the story about the farmer who was showing his wife how his donkey always listens when he speaks softly to him. He told the donkey to go, but the donkey didn't move. Finally, the farmer hit him in the head with a board and the donkey went. His wife said, "You told me he listens when you speak softly to him." He said, "He does! But sometimes I have to get his attention first!"

God speaks softly to us. But if we are not listening, sometimes he has to get our attention first. (Again, we cannot say that Job wasn't listening, but no doubt God's refining is easier when we are listening.) God's ways are bigger than ours, beyond finding out. But as we rest in Him, we will find that we will soar as eagles, who don't even flap their wings, but simply glide on the wind! (Isaiah 40:10-31.)

Everything in our lives comes down to hearing His voice.

God is Sovereign – All the Time

Rob through his ministry works closely with the families of children with life-threatening illnesses. There is hardly a more humbling experience than to watch a child struggle with cancer and the horrific treatments that go with it. There is hardly a more baffling experience than to watch one child recover and another child not recover.

Likewise, I know of a family who left their baby in the car, each parent thinking the other had gotten her out. By the time they realized she was in the car, she was dead. I too once left my Hannah in the car. A friend had met me at my house, and we got busy talking in the kitchen. Chris, who was nine, asked where Hannah was. Even then it did not dawn on me she was still in the car. I figured she was playing with her sister. He said, "I'm going to find Hannah." He found her in the car, hot and groggy. I began crying in gratitude that despite my mistake, God had rescued Hannah.

We can hardly help asking, *Why did He save Hannah and not the other baby? Why did He heal one cancer child and not the other?*

I cannot pretend to understand or explain why some prayers are answered the way we want and some aren't – whatever cataclysmic event we are facing. As tempted as we may be to point to the obedience of one and not the other, we are blasphemous to say that our behavior brought either result.

I can only turn to Jesus when he was asked if the man was born blind because of his sin or his parents' sin (John 9:1-3): "It was neither that this man sinned, nor his parents; but it was so that the works of God might be displayed in him." We are faced with trusting God to be sovereign in the good times and the heartbreaking times.

Heartwork

1. What scope and sequence do you see in the events of your life?
2. Can you see how much you have grown through events that appeared random at the time?
3. What scope and sequence do you see in your children's lives? That is, how has God used "random" events to develop their knowledge of Him?
4. Can you see ways God has revealed Himself to you and/or your children through difficult circumstances?
5. Are you willingly giving God the title deed to your children?
6. Ask the Lord where you may be stuck, having difficulty surrendering your life or your children's lives to Him. (Perhaps you have found it difficult to trust God through a tough time.) He will be faithful to show you.
7. Ask the Lord to encourage you through this challenging process.

• • •

chapter 7
GOD BLESS THE BROKEN ROAD

*"It is doubtful whether God can bless a man
greatly until He has hurt him deeply." -A.W. Tozer*

*"One thing about brokenness that God taught me the other day.
In Revelation 21:4, it says that Jesus will wipe away every tear
from our eyes, and when I read that, I knew that I wanted to have
many genuine tears for Him to wipe away, that my brokenness
will bring me closer to Him now and later."* Annie Cottrell

*"Every long lost dream led me to where you are. Others who broke
my heart, they were like northern stars, pointing me on my way into
Your loving arms. This much I know is true, that God blessed the
broken road that led me straight to You."* Rascal Flatts, Broken Road

*"Thank you for letting me fall off my bike – and
making me wear a helmet!"* College student to parents

I have a question for you. Let's pretend God said to you, "You know all those dreams you have for your child? Everything your heart desires for them on this earth? They are not going to happen. None of them. Instead I'm calling him to be single and poor in… some remote place. But your child will know Me deeply, intimately, and be completely satisfied in Me. Would you be happy with that?" I think it would be terribly difficult to answer yes to that question – for ourselves, or for our children.

So God says, "Alright, let Me put it this way: I will accomplish every dream you have for your child – career, marriage, children, friends – everything. But your child will never hear from Me. What about that?" Doesn't your heart leap and say, "No, *NO!* Nothing is worth not knowing You!"

How much God means to us and how much we trust Him is really the heart of what we value. We say we love Him and trust Him, but deep down, many of us fear that the worst possible scenario we can imagine is the life He's going to give us. But that is a lie from the enemy! Jesus says in Matthew 7:11: "If you then, being evil, know how to give good gifts to your children, how much more will your Father who is in heaven give what is good to those who ask Him!"

David says in Psalm 37:4: "Delight yourself in the LORD; And He will give you the desires of your heart."

God placed our fondest dreams in our hearts and longs to fulfill them, just as we long to fulfill our children's fondest dreams. But He wants us to put Him first.

Missionary Amy Carmichael said: "…although God requires all to be put on the altar, He doesn't necessarily take all of it." That means He just wants us to bring all those dreams to the table and surrender them to Him.

It also means that we're going to have to be broken by the Lord. A thoroughbred stallion is a powerful breed, but he must be broken and learn to respond to the bit in his mouth and the direction of his master – or he is useless. God does the same thing to us.

Brokenness is really the toughest and lowest points of our scope and sequence.

A mom was telling me how committed she is to protecting her young girls from life – she doesn't want anything bad to happen to them. Her heart's desire is to protect them – of course! I said, "When did you come to the Lord: during easy times or hard times? [Pause] And when did you grow in the Lord most: during fun times or difficult times?" She smiled.

"Yeah, but don't some kids grow up in Christian homes and

not have struggles?" she asked. I answered that our kids must struggle in order to know God for themselves. It may be an external or internal struggle, more extreme or less extreme, but they must grow into and adjust to this relationship with God for Him to become their own. Otherwise, they're just borrowing from their parents. The struggle is the *means* to know God's faithfulness.

We want our children to know God's faithfulness, His lovingkindness, His grace, His power. But we don't want them to go through the situations that grow those qualities in them. How do people learn those things? When there are situations that require Him to come through (when our strengths and talents fail)!

Consider John 11. Mary and Martha sent for Jesus when Lazarus was dying. John 11:4-6 says: "But when Jesus heard this, He said, 'This sickness is not to end in death, but for the glory of God, so that the Son of God may be glorified by it.' Now Jesus loved Martha and her sister and Lazarus. So when He heard that he was sick, *He then stayed two days longer in the place where He was*" (emphasis added).

Haven't we been in situations where Jesus took just a little longer than we thought was necessary? Didn't we feel abandoned? Like He was not coming at all?

He tarried. He took His time. And then, after Lazarus was dead, He showed up. And the sisters are kind of like, *Uh, it's a little late*. Martha says: "Lord, if You had been here, my brother would not have died. Even now I know that whatever You ask of God, God will give You" (v. 21-22).

Martha is understandably upset, and she wants to trust Him, she does trust Him, but Lazarus is dead. "Jesus said to her, 'Your brother will rise again.' Martha said to Him, 'I know that he will rise again in the resurrection on the last day'" (v. 23-24). The thought of Jesus raising Lazarus from the dead was not even in her realm of possibility. By the way, Jesus did not chide her for this. How gentle He is to us!

"Jesus said to her, 'I am the resurrection and the life; he who believes in Me will live even if he dies, and everyone who lives and believes in Me will never die.' Do you believe this?" (v. 25).

We want Him to rush in and fix it before it gets too horrible. But He does not. He often waits longer than we think is bearable. Haven't we all been there? But He is waiting for something to be fully realized that is bigger than we expected.

The story goes on to say that because Lazarus actually died, the Jews came to mourn for him and to comfort the family. So not only does Jesus raise Lazarus from the dead, which is an incredible feat all by itself, but all those Jews, who wouldn't have otherwise been there, were able to witness this amazing thing and come to believe in Him. This was "for the glory of God," (v. 40) just as He said.

> "Don't ever be ashamed of your testimony, because that is how God led you to Him."

Think back over your life in the Lord and all the twists and turns it has taken. Did everything go in a straight line? Or did you take a winding path, even a "broken road" as the song says? Think of the twists and turns that revealed Him to you, that deepened your faith, that showed you things about Him that you could not have seen any other way. Do you see it? Our walks are a unique and personal treasure – because that is how He reveals Himself to us.

Though I came to the Lord at fourteen, I took the scenic route through my twenties before I came to complete dependence on Him. I was embarrassed revealing to my dear friend the painful mistakes I'd made during those years. She wisely and generously said to me: "Don't ever be ashamed of your testimony, because that is how God led you to Him." What a relief that was to me! I wouldn't trade my pain – none of it – for what I've learned about the Lord. Not a chance. Is that true for you too?

We have to allow our children the same privilege and not try to protect them from everything. God doesn't protect them from everything, and He loves them more than we do. Brokenness is a good thing. When do we learn that a hot stove really burns? When we touch it.

Being broken is the process of removing our crutches so we see for ourselves how lame we really are. 2 Corinthians 12:8-9 says: "Concerning this [the thorn in his flesh] I implored the Lord three times that it might leave me. And He has said to me, 'My grace is sufficient for you, for power is perfected in weakness.' Most gladly, therefore, I will rather boast about my weaknesses, so that the power of Christ may dwell in me. Therefore I am well content with weaknesses, with insults, with distresses, with persecutions, with difficulties, for Christ's sake; *for when I am weak, then I am strong*'" (emphasis added).

God's power is perfected in our weakness. When we are weak, then we are strong. A dear friend started crying during worship at church. Afterward she said, "I shouldn't cry – I'm a leader. I need to have it all together." Do you hear the burden she is carrying? And the lie that comes from satan? I don't blame her, because many of us Christians, deep down, expect that in each other (though we don't say it). Her desire was to encourage women by allowing them to see her strength. But the truth is, we need to see other's weaknesses – and our own weaknesses – because then we see *God's* strength!

As much as I love my friend, I don't want her strength – I want God's strength! We all do this, I'm afraid; it's inherent in the fall, the desire to be like God. That is why God has to break us. To pull ourselves together and do our best is *bondage*, because then only our strength emerges. When we fall apart, into the Lord, we see *His* strength – and it's far, *far* greater than ours, far greater than anything we could come up with. We might be able to save Lazarus with rest or medicine – but Jesus can raise him from the dead!!

This theme of brokenness is throughout the Bible. Moses – remember the forty years in the wilderness, before he ever led the Israelites out of Egypt? David – with Bathsheba, and his sons' rebellion. Peter – all the times he spoke in haste and when he denied Jesus. Paul – who killed many Christians "for God." The Bible is full of people who have been broken. It's not that these people are not strong enough, not showing enough resolve – these failings are *by design*, to bring them to dependence on God. If we were not destined to fail in our own power, then how would we know our need for a Savior? How grateful I am that God revealed to me my weakness, and let me fall, so I would let *Him* stand – for me!

Jesus went through testing too, spending forty days in the wilderness (whereas the Jews' breaking took forty *years*!). But He alone did not need to be broken, which His wilderness experience revealed, because His will was submitted wholly to God from the start.

What about you? How has God broken you? Has He used events in your life to show you His sovereignty, His trustworthiness, and that your own methods are not sufficient?

We went through a horrendous time when we lived in Texas some years back. We found out that a babysitter (a nursery worker and children's ministry volunteer in our church) was a child molester. We were horrified. It was more than we ever thought we would have to face – and we didn't understand how it could happen. We had to go to court as witnesses. We were overwhelmed and could not begin to see how God was going to redeem the situation. (Perhaps, like Martha facing Lazarus' tomb, we did not think it was possible.)

Rob had a friend in ministry who ran a family counseling center in Phoenix. The Lord tenderly led us to drive there as a family. We were able to get intensive counseling as a family, and it turned a whole new page in our lives! After one daylong counseling session, Rob and I sat by the hotel pool, watching the kids fall back in the water, the orange and purple Phoenix sun setting behind them. We looked at each other, so grateful, because God was doing something huge for us: He was restoring relationships in our family, helping us walk through forgiveness and healing our wounds. At the end of it all, God moved us to Phoenix! We could not have predicted that God would turn such a terrible experience (with this pedophile) into something wonderful. He used it to show us His power, His strength and His sovereignty.

As it happened, our pastor had just been teaching about brokenness. (Looking back, we see how God had been preparing us.) The best part is that once we realized God was breaking us, it became much easier to take – it really did. As this whole ordeal began, our pastor recommended Gene Edwards' allegory, *Tale of Three Kings*. In it, we learned that we can react to bad news in various ways. We can dig in our heels, set up resistance and make things as difficult as possible (as Saul did by lashing out in violent anger against his perceived enemy, David, and even against his own son, Jonathan). We can react by taking matters into our own hands and trying to bring about our own will (as Absalom did when he began a coup against his father, King David). Or we can see every element, every event as from the Lord's own hand, trust in Him and rest in Him, regardless of how out of control things look (as David did by not killing Saul when he had opportunity, though Saul had already tried several times to kill him). These responses show us how much we trust God. And they shape the outcome of the story. (Saul ended in shame and death, Absalom ended dying in the coup he began, and David received the kingship from God, ruling over it well – though imperfectly – for many years.)

> But once we understood God was sovereign even over that, we stopped flailing...

David's response was strengthened because He trusted God to have the situation completely in hand. David's hallmark of teachability was to see God's hand in everything that came his way. When a descendent of Saul was throwing stones at David and cursing him, one of his mighty men wanted to go cut his head off. David is the *king!* But David said, "Leave him alone, and let him curse me because the Lord told him to do this" (2 Samuel

16:11). That is one teachable king.

As we went through the trial, we had a hard time seeing God's sovereignty when we saw people make what we thought were poor decisions (the pedophile's family, and the church elders over him, for instance). But once we understood God was sovereign even over that, we stopped flailing, we stopped wondering why this was happening. We just sat still and let God do what He wanted to do.

Sometimes we cannot imagine that the things He is allowing He is actually going to work together for our good, as Romans 8:28 tells us. Children being molested? Our neighbor's honor-roll student getting pregnant? A friend dying of cancer? It's hard to imagine any of those events possibly being for our good. But when God walks you through it, you see what He can do (usually after you have reached the other side).

Heartwork

1. Where has the Lord broken you in the past? How did He grow you into the image of Christ through it?
2. Where has God broken your children?
3. Is He breaking you or your children right now?
4. Ask Him what He is showing you through all the struggle.
5. Does your teen have a problem you would like to help solve?
6. Ask the Lord to show you what He is accomplishing through the problem.
7. Can you see how the worst things have become the best things, because of what God accomplished through it?

• • •

chapter 8
RESPECTING THEIR JOURNEY

> "Plant a turnip. Get a turnip. Maybe you'll
> get two. That's why I love vegetables;
> You know that they'll come through!... While with children,
> it's bewilderin'. You don't know until the seed is nearly grown
> – just what you've sown." Plant a Radish, The Fantasticks

> "You take the defeat and somehow put it in your line of life
> and figure out that it will make you better and tougher."
> Al Trautwig, commentating on women's gymnastics

> "You've got to be a man about things and suck it up!"
> Alicia Sacramone, elite women's gymnast

> "This isn't my family's journey, or my pastor's
> journey. This is my journey." Tabitha, Marathon Runner

Growing kids is like growing plants. We put seeds into the soil, provide water, sunlight, and even fertilizer – but God grows the plant. The gardener's biggest job is to keep the bugs, weeds and animals away from the plant so it can thrive. So it is with children. We plant them, we water them, we nurture them, we even provide the fertilizer – but God grows them. The best thing we can do is to protect them (from a variety of predators) and provide for them (physically, spiritually, emotionally) while God grows them.

When you go buy seeds, you pick the kind you want. But when

you have kids, you don't get to pick. You may be hoping for children as beautiful as red roses that will dress the table, match your décor, and smell sweet – but you may get marigolds. They don't match and they don't smell so sweet! But God made *those* children and gave them to you in His perfect plan. That child of yours may not become the missionary you hoped for, but a bartender! Yet, a bartender may be exactly what God called him to be. We want what we want, but we get what we get. As my niece used to say: "You get what you get and you don't throw a fit!" Many parents have trouble accepting the children God gave them for who they are… and most problems that come up in counseling seem to be with people who did not feel accepted for who they are.

God gave all of us feelings, preferences and views of the world. Just because our children are less experienced and less mature than we are does not mean that we should not honor their feelings, preferences and views of the world. To do less than that is to push them into a corner, to exasperate them, and to hinder them from unfolding as God designed them.

> …if we do not respect our children's choices, we will drive them to frustration and to hiding things from us.

Our children say they are full, but we tell them to clean their plate. We feel cold and tell our child to put on a sweater.

Marie's mother made her drink milk every morning. She noticed her stomach hurt after she drank milk. But her mother told her that milk can't give anyone a tummyache and she would have to drink it. "So," Marie said to me, "I'd pretend to drink it and pour it out." Righteous or not, justifiable or not, it is *true* that if we do not respect our children's choices, we will drive them to frustration and to hiding things from us.

The NY Times bestselling book, *The Gift of Fear*, by Gavin deBecker, describes how in most crimes, there were warning signs along the way that our intuition understands, but our reason talks us out of. That is, we may recognize fear, but because we don't understand why we are afraid, we dismiss it. We say, *don't be so silly – why would you think such a thing?* By the time our reason catches up with our intuition, it is too late to escape. Our intuition is there to protect us, but we do not listen, and we pay the price.

God gives us intuition – and His leading – to protect us. We reason it all away at our own peril. Do not overpower your child's intuition, preferences, or heart's desires. (I'm not saying, *he feels like going to the waterpark today, so we're going to the waterpark.* I'm saying, *he says milk gives him a tummyache, so I won't make him drink milk.* Or, *she strongly objects to this babysitter, so I'm going to find a different babysitter.*)

Not respecting our children's hearts instills self-doubt and fear. Many parents try to control their children's crying by shaming or punishing them when they cry. But they need to cry. Crying is part of the human design, even if it causes discomfort in the parent who wants to fix the situation and can't. I met with two gals in one weekend; both came through families in which they were punished for crying. Now when they do need to cry, they cannot, and it gives them migraine headaches.

When we respect our children as people, we stand ready to listen to the big questions in life that they want to come to us for. My husband Rob had gym class last period in school, and in the shower he overheard classmates talking about sex. He wanted to ask his dad something about it. He waited for his dad to pick him up so they could talk, and the first thing his dad said was, "Your hair's still wet! You have to dry your hair after your shower." At that moment, he decided not to ask his dad the question. In fact, something shifted in him and he decided not to talk to his dad about sex at all.

We must guide, of course, but it can be after greeting the child we haven't seen all day. We can say hello first. In this case, a "hello" would have kept the door open long enough for Rob to ask and for him and his dad to have a much more important conversation than his wet hair. We want to be ready to hear. Then we can offer the guidance and support we have for them, and that they need from us. But they need us to remember it's their journey.

They Choose Their Journey

Olympic women's gymnastics thrills me! Every four years, we watch the championships, the trials, the Olympics and the stories of the athletes. I am always awed by the young women's dedication and commitment. These gymnasts spend their childhoods perfecting their sport to become the best in the world, suffering injuries and setbacks as well as enjoying great accomplishments. Sacrifice and dedication to this degree come only from within. The highly dedicated coaches and parents play vital roles, but what they cannot do is make the investment that only the gymnast herself brings to her achievement.

Most teen's stories are not as dramatic or as publicly visible as an Olympic gymnast's, but they too are on personal journeys that only they can achieve. They too will suffer injuries and setbacks as well as accomplishments. They too make investments in hopes of a good return. We can support them, encourage them and counsel them, but we cannot force them down a path, and we cannot walk it for them.

God has their journey mapped out; our part is to respect them enough to let Him work in them; their part will be to own their journey.

Here is how God parents us: He offers us His Son, and we may accept or decline His offer. We cannot defer that decision to anyone else. God could force us to accept salvation, but then it would be meaningless. To have meaning, we must choose it of our own will.

God also does not force our children to choose His journey. Free choice is important enough that God gives it to them in this area, too. We honor God and our children by likewise allowing that choice.

How Does God Speak to Us?

So how does God entice us to choose the journey He offers us? Well, it's in the way He treats us. God doesn't attack His children. When we are His (through Jesus), he treats us like sons and daughters, not like orphans in the street.

Contrast that to our enemy, who constantly wages war against us. He prowls around as a roaring lion, seeking whom he may devour. This contrast is extremely helpful in determining the source of the voice in your head. If it is encouraging, loving, life-giving, you can be sure it is the Lord. (The enemy never talks to you that way.) If it is specific conviction that offers hope, a way out, then it is from the Lord.

The Lord says things like: "Well done. Good job. You have grown so much. I love you." And when we need correcting, He says things like: "You were too harsh to your daughter and you didn't listen to her. You need to seek her forgiveness."

If the voice is condemning, harsh and driving, you can rest assured it is the enemy seeking whom he may devour. If it is generally condemning (rather than specifically convicting), it is from the enemy. The Lord never talks to us that way. The enemy says things like: "That was a stupid thing to do. You've been making that same stupid mistake for twenty years. There is no hope for you." He will say, "You were harsh with your daughter. Again. You're a terrible mother."

You may think I'm exaggerating, but if you listen to those stray thoughts, you will see they sound like this. Where do you think they come from? It's not from God – He would never say that to His beloved child, created in His image. It sounds like your voice, but that is because the enemy speaks to you in your voice. Also, the enemy has been saying roughly the same condemning thing to you all these years; you would naturally assume it comes from you. Understanding this is helpful in our own walk with the Lord, so that we do not succumb to the enemy, so that we do not lose hope.

This is also helpful in talking with our children. Remember that our children hear the enemy's voice in their head all day long, just as we do. They have to battle thoughts of unworthiness, ineptitude, as fully as we do. That is what the enemy does. He isn't out shopping for new jeans; he's seeking to devour as many people as he can.

If we want to parent our children as God parents us, we need to be encouraging, loving, life-giving. We can correct specifically rather than condemn generally.

Rob has had to help me in this area. When my kids fail to do something I specifically asked them to do, I get personally offended. It took a long time for me to see this, but I react as if I can't *believe* they did not put the dishes away after I told them to. (How many things have I not done that I was supposed to?)

But consider how we react to problem situations. I recently got a speeding ticket, and let me tell you, it tormented me. The fine, the possible points – driver's school? It was torture. Would my repentance have increased or the situation been improved if my husband "chewed me up" over it? Absolutely not. I was already tormenting myself. What I needed, and got (and fully appreciated) was his love and support.

When our kids mess up, they need our love and support. Sin carries its own consequences. Especially if they are repentant, they do not need us to "chew them up." If they are not repentant, we need to seek the Lord about how to handle it. I have gotten more than one speeding ticket over the years – which means I have continued to speed even after receiving a ticket. But finally, after many years, I have gotten better about watching my speed. I know some people shake their heads at this! Consider it my area of weakness. (If you don't generally speed, think of the area in which you do struggle – you will see what I mean.) We don't learn our tough lessons overnight. Even though those tickets tortured me, I had to learn the lesson myself over time.

Our children likewise need to see the cost of their sin and come to repentance. Still, the Lord convicts specifically, and He also provides a way out, so that we can stand (1 Corinthians 10:13). And the Lord is able to make us stand (1 Jude 24). I am so grateful.

My point here is that the enemy constantly wages war. We are never in reprieve. We must focus on the relationship with the Lord, because only His power will sustain us in battle. The behavior comes along after the heart is changed. Some of your behavior and mine did not change for some time after our hearts changed. Our job is to be patient, and kind, and loving, while God does His amazing work in our children.

They're in Training

Training our children to listen to God's voice is a long, long process that requires our patience and respect. When my children were quite young, I would send them to ask the Lord about decisions they needed to make. That is how I made my decisions, and no one had told me you couldn't train your kids to trust the Lord for themselves.

> "Don't trust yourself to hear Him; trust Him to speak to you."

I was at the store with one of my Lego-aficionados, who felt compelled to buy a certain new Lego set. Well, he had freedom to spend his own money (within certain boundaries), but I would always suggest he pray about it. More often than not, he would say that the Lord told him that it was his choice! Of course. But that did not worry me then, and even less does it now. Because I was not teaching whether or not to buy a Lego set; I was teaching how to hear the Lord. And in the fullness of time, that is what my children learned. In the beginning, of course, they don't really hear *No* from Him because they don't really want to hear *No*. As they grew, they would begin to say, "God doesn't really want me to do that."

Secular parenting advice includes letting your children make decisions of limited consequence early (what to wear to school, for instance), so they can learn to make decisions. My Christian advice is to let them seek the Lord for themselves early so they train their heart to hear Him. They will miss-hear Him sometimes; I still do, too. But the process of learning His voice is what's valuable here.

And as my friend, author Jennifer Kennedy Dean says: "Don't trust yourself to hear Him; trust Him to speak to you."

There are some parameters here, of course, and their "answer from the Lord" is not always permission. As decisions became more consequential, I would also pray (or Rob and I would), for God to speak to us, too. That helps confirm the decision. But don't worry trying to prevent every mistake – it is easy for them to hear what they want to hear from God. But they will grow and learn. That is what this training opportunity is all about.

A friend's daughter just today got her hand slammed in the car door. I think all of my kids have done it. You can tell your child not to put their hand on the doorjamb, because it can get slammed in the door, but they forget because they don't realize the danger. But once it gets slammed, they don't do it again. That's how learning works.

Heartwork

1. Is your child turning out differently than you hoped? It may be tough to admit, but are you disappointed in your child? Talk to the Lord about it.
2. Have you diminished your child's intuition, preferences and heart's desires? Again, even if it's tough to admit, talk to the Lord about it.
3. What path is your child interested it? What delights his heart (athletics, writing, theater, science, public speaking, mathematics)?
4. How is God calling you to come alongside them in that interest? (I am not saying teens already know the direction their lives will take – most do not. I'm saying whatever path is ahead they will have to own – you can only support them in it, but you cannot own it for them.)

5. Are you allowing and encouraging them to hear the Lord for themselves? How would the Lord lead you to grow in that ability?

∙ ∙ ∙

chapter 9
MAN LOOKS AT THE OUTWARD APPEARANCE

"Man looks at the outward appearance, but the Lord looks at the heart." 1 Samuel 16:7

"The truth will out." Unknown

Outward Appearance - People-Pleasing

The doctor told the young mom concerned about her son's toilet training: "Oh, he'll be trained before he goes to college." About his baby speech: "Oh, he'll speak fine before he goes to

> We often assess our children...forgetting that they are not yet grown, not yet matured, not yet where they will be when they leave home.

college." About his walking: "Oh, he'll walk before he goes to college." A new mother can be so worried about her baby "turning out alright," while the doctor has seen lots and lots of babies turn out just fine.

We often assess our children according to how they look to us right now, forgetting that they are not yet grown, not yet matured, not yet where they will be when they leave home. Worse, we often assess our children according to how they look to others...or how we're afraid they look to others.

Our job is to remember that God is doing a work in them. I

think of the old high school reunion cliché: the football player had become a coach potato and the nerd now owns his own company. The cheerleader's beauty has faded while the ugly ducking has become a swan.

I'm obviously using a broad brush, but clichés usually carry some truth. The truth is that we do not always recognize inner beauty, the late bloomer needs a chance to bloom, and what draws or repels us on the outside is not always the whole story. And, certainly we do not know what God is doing in a person's life.

When the prophet Samuel came to Jesse's house to find among his sons the one God had appointed as the next king, Jesse did not even bring his youngest in from tending the sheep, as he did not consider him a contender. Yet, Samuel persisted until he found David and anointed him as king.

We find it difficult not to categorize, assessing this one as musical, that one as logical, this one as brainy and that one as beautiful. We can hardly help it. On the positive side, we can use our intuition about their bents to help guide them by nurturing their talents or correcting their liabilities. It is worth noting the artistic ability you saw in your baby at age three. But *how* will God use that talent? We don't know. We can only encourage them in the Lord, trusting that He will draw and lead them into something we could not have seen. Jesse would never have said David was "king" material, yet David became a man after God's own heart, the king for whose sake God showed favor to all his descendents.

But we have to be very careful in assessing our children, because we can pull them down like no one else can. We can also develop such high expectations that they feel pressed to measure up. This can easily trip them up. Even our positive assessments of their abilities can unwittingly pressure them to continue to measure up. We look at the outward appearance, but only the Lord fully knows the heart.

My grilled chicken looks succulent and delicious, but inside it is sometimes either dry or undercooked. My friend's grilled chicken looks the same as mine, but inside it is tender and moist. Things are not always as they seem.

Look back over your years as a parent and think back on all the many successes you've had. Can you recall some fabulous times? Do you see how much you've grown as a parent?

> I look back at my children and see individual threads of work God has done.

Now think back on your mistakes. You might join me in saying: "I'll take parental blunders for $200, Alex." It takes awhile to learn to parent. Aren't you grateful for God's kindness, forgiveness and grace? Our children are growing through similar difficulty in learning to navigate this adult world with its increased requirements and responsibilities. They need the same grace as they too are growing and refining.

But they *are* growing and refining!

I look back at my children and see individual threads of work God has done. He used mundane events to draw them to Him and small decisions to teach them to trust Him.

I'd like to paint a little picture of how God lines out our unique journeys, and there are as many journeys as there are people.

When our oldest son, Chris, was nine, he was just going to bed one night when he asked Rob how we know that Christianity is true. How do we know we're right? Rob began explaining the many prophecies that point to Christ and the personal relationship we have with Him. Rob did not panic at the question. It is a good question for a thinking person, and Chris was at a good age for rigorous thought. He had begun to wonder whether his acceptance of Christ at age three was real, another good question. Three is still the age of magical thinking – it is fair to reevaluate a decision made at that age.

They talked through it, and Chris simply asked the Lord again, from his increased maturity. I believe that he responded at age three to what he understood. Then as he gained understanding, he responded more fully. We need not be afraid of rigorous thought. Does his question about knowing God mean he doesn't believe? No, it means he is wrestling with deeper understanding. God is not offended or dismayed by our questions. We need not doubt a conversion at age three. But how like God to work a deeper understanding in this boy, so his relationship continues to mature instead of becoming "something I did when I was three." He continues to assimilate his increased maturity, wisdom and experience.

> God saved us once from hell into heaven, but He is saving us daily from the hellish evil of the world.

God is trustworthy with His children, and we can let ourselves trust Him. Paul says in Philippians 2:12: "Work out your own salvation with fear and trembling." That means to work with it to see how tenacious it is, what's it's made of and what this incredible thing is that God has given us. Our salvation is simply unfathomable, and salvation includes being saved from hell into heaven – but the word is used much *more often* in the Bible to mean the continued deliverance from this evil world in which we find ourselves.

God saved us once from hell into heaven, but He is saving us daily from the hellish evil of the world.

To put it another way: God is always interested in working out what He has put in us. When we come to Him for the very first time, He gives us all we need – just like a baby has everything in him to be a boy, a man, a father, a grandfather – it's all in there, but it's not all fully matured or "worked out." Colossians 2:10 says: "...you are complete in Him..." So when we come to Him, we have all we need, but we must let Him be fully revealed in us.

Hebrews 2:10 says something very interesting: "For it was fitting for Him, for whom are all things, and through whom are all things, in bringing many sons to glory, to *perfect* the author of their salvation [Jesus] through sufferings" (emphasis added). How will God perfect Jesus when He is already perfect? "To perfect" here means "to mature." So God matured, or completed, Jesus through His sufferings. (Just as Jesus "grew in wisdom," so also did God mature Him.) That gives me great comfort indeed. My sufferings are definitely for the purpose of maturing me in Christ; they are not random, nor are they punishment for my misbehavior.

My daughter Annie's journey is a great picture of how God prepares us for what He calls us to. Annie is naturally an introvert, but God has some plans for her that require her to be more extraverted, so He's been working that out in her. He used three specific instances that required her trust in Him, and she had a choice each time whether she was going to trust Him. When she was fourteen, older brother Chris had organized a big game at the park with their friends. Annie desperately wanted to participate, but she was afraid. *What if I'm no good at it? What if the other kids don't want me there? What if I look like an idiot?* Aren't those kinds of things our teens wrestle with? I asked her what the Lord was telling her. She said God told her to trust Him and go for it. She participated and – of course – had a great time.

The next incident was when she wanted to go to a one-week worldview class, but the class was already full. The director said, "If she will just come to it, almost certainly someone will have to cancel for some reason, and there will be room for her. But I can't promise that." So we were faced with driving the three hours there, getting excited, and then there may or may not be a place for her. We both prayed, but the Lord wouldn't assure her there was a place. He *did* say to trust Him. Now this is bigger than it sounds for a young teen, because she risked showing up eager to be there, seeing everyone, and then having to turn around and go home. Even many adults would be uncomfortable. She finally knew that God was asking her to take the risk. She even rode with her friends, which increased her investment in going, and the embarrassment if she were turned away. I felt confident that God had a place for her – but this was her battle, not mine. (I have my own battles.) What do you think happened? A girl was sick and couldn't come – she had a spot! And it was a great event for her.

> God has a path for them, and though we don't know the end from the beginning, He does.

The third challenge was when she was invited to intern for six months for a Christian political group – *in Georgia*. She was sixteen. It was also a challenge for Mom and Dad to let her go! But we thought it was a great opportunity for her; it dovetailed nicely with the internship she had already lined up for the spring. But it was a big step for our girl. Well, she went, and had a spectacular experience – tough and exhausting – but growing. It also helped prepare her for her spring internship.

My whole point with all of this is that God has a path for them, and though we don't know the end from the beginning, He does.

Of course, I didn't know God was putting these elements together in succession to give her confidence to do what *He* had planned for her. These appeared to be isolated events until we were looking back at them. In fact, she is the one who pointed out the sequence of events. Proverbs 16:9 says: "The mind of man plans his way, But the LORD directs his steps."

Herein lies the trouble with being a "fruit inspector" (as in, "I won't judge anyone, but I can inspect their fruit"). I don't know what God is doing in someone enough to judge his fruit. I've jumped to plenty of conclusions, but I've turned out to be wrong enough that now I lean more toward Romans 14:4, which tells me not to judge another man's servant.

If we want fruit, Jesus tells us how to get fruit: "I am the vine, you are the branches; he who abides in Me and I in him, he bears much fruit, for apart from Me you can do nothing" (John 15:5). What does a grape have to do to grow in the vine? Stay connected.

That's all. It doesn't have to labor; doesn't have to worry about finding water. The vinedresser will provide everything – from sunshine to fertilizer. We just rest in Him, and He will do the work in us.

Our job is to trust God 100% with our teens. That means letting go of our own agenda in favor of God's agenda. And whether we can relax and trust God with this precious little one of ours says a lot about how much we trust God. Our job is also to accept our teen 100%. Parenting is about following the Lord.

Heartwork

1. Ask God to show you that His love for you has nothing to do with your actions.
2. Ask God where you are parenting for your child's best interest, and where you are parenting to "look good." (Don't worry – we've all been there.)
3. Ask the Lord where you are parenting to meet your child's needs, and where you are parenting to meet your own needs. (We've all been here, too.)
4. What threads has God been weaving into your child's life?
5. Can you see a pattern to the path your child has been on? Ask the Lord to show you.
6. Have you been trying to conform your child's outward appearance? Ask the Lord to help you see his heart.
7. Ask the Lord what He wants to show you from this chapter.

• • •

chapter 10
LOVING THE PRODIGAL

> "And not many days later, the younger son gathered everything together and went on a journey into a distant country, and there he squandered his estate with loose living." Luke 15:13

> "And he would have gladly filled his stomach with the pods that the swine were eating, and no one was giving anything to him." Luke 15:16

> "'Quickly bring out the best robe and put it on him, and put a ring on his hand and sandals on his feet; and bring the fattened calf, kill it, and let us eat and celebrate; for this son of mine was dead and has come to life again; he was lost and has been found.'" Luke 15:22-24

God is at Work

So far, we've talked about when things are going well. But sometimes our children rebel.

> He did not finally replace our desperately wicked heart with a *new* desperately wicked heart, but with a good heart.

The foundation to stand on is this: if your child has accepted Christ as his Savior, he is now a new creation. Ezekiel 36:26 tells us that the new heart is *good*. When we became Christians, God made us new creations, with good, redeemed hearts, and sin no longer suits us. Jesus died on the cross, rose from the dead and now offers us new life in Him. He did not finally replace our desperately wicked heart with a *new* desperately wicked heart, but with a good heart.

Sin carries its own consequences, and the sins that we committed prior to Christ, which did not bother us then, bother us more now even if no one else knows it.

When we are learning something, we are often happy to skip steps, but God is thorough, and steps that seem unnecessary to us are part of God's scope and sequence. The same goes for our child, and we can take heart that He has them in His hands.

When I was in my twenties, doing what was right in my own eyes, the Holy Spirit was convicting me from within. No one knew that. I told no one and my actions gave no hint. My poor sister who prayed for me without ceasing thought I would never come back to my senses. That is how things appear with the prodigal. We see nothing, and we get frustrated and heart-broken, but God is working.

While we are tempted to look at the rebel and wonder if he ever accepted Christ in the first place, a valid question, we need to understand that many Christians, who have truly accepted the Lord, go through periods of rebellion – sometimes extended periods. An observer then would have doubted that I had ever accepted Christ. While it's true that someone may not have actually accepted Christ, it is also true that they may have rejected what they had accepted heartily at one time (and are dismayed about the voice is still convicting them from within).

Sin is an Illegitimate Means to Meet Legitimate Needs

Spiderman is a hero who constantly saves people from evil. So it's pretty scary in the third movie when that black goop gets inside him and turns him bad. Here's the part I loved. Peter Parker (Spiderman) is going into his apartment and the landlord stops him to tell him his rent is late. Peter snaps back at him rudely, telling him that he will get his rent when the lock on the door is fixed, as he disappears into his apartment. The landlord is aghast. As he opens his mouth, you expect him to say, "He has done it now, he is so rude, he is so evicted." That's what most of us would say. But he surprises us all, including his daughter standing next to him, when he says: "He is a good person. He must be in big trouble."

I think I cried. How perceptive. And how true it is in real life, that someone uncharacteristically lashes out in anger when something is wrong. But how seldom we recognize it. Instead we get offended by the behavior and lash back ourselves. How much better it would be to find out what is driving the problem.

We continue to sin, even though our heart has been made new, even though sin no longer suits us. I believe that is largely because *sin is an illegitimate means to meet legitimate needs.*

Our teens' need for love and belonging are legitimate; sex, drinking, drugs, and gangs to meet those needs are illegitimate. Wanting to feel valued and respected is legitimate; ridiculing someone else so you feel more valuable is illegitimate. Knowing this helps tremendously in being able to get to the root cause of our sin.

By age twenty-four, I had already endured a tumultuous childhood and the deaths of both parents and three brothers. I went off to New York where I began "doing what was right in my own eyes," putting behind me the faith that had sustained me through high school. But my faithful sister, Karin, had faith on my behalf. She prayed for me diligently, and boy did I need it! She knew I was in rebellion, though she didn't know half of what I was doing.

Also, the Holy Spirit was living in me as I struggled through this time. I might have appeared to be indifferent to my sin – as it might appear to be with your teens or young adults – but if they are Christians, the Spirit is convicting them.

Our kids have a huge job of maturing and trying to make sense of the world around them and their place in it. They need us to have faith in God *for* them. Sin carries its own consequences. Though they justify it to your face, God is convicting their hearts.

"Faith is the substance of things hopes for, the evidence of things not seen" (Hebrews 11:1). Remember, the goal of parenting is to point our kids to their God, that they may come to love Him with all their heart, soul, mind and strength (and love others as themselves).

> They need us to have faith in God for them.

During this time of praying, Karin happened to lose the diamond from her ring. She searched and searched for days, and finally she pleaded with the Lord to have the angels get her diamond wherever it was and return it to her. The next day, the diamond was sitting on top of her bed – the bed she'd slept in and made. She burst into tears. Then she heard the Lord say, as clear as can be, "Karin! Don't you think Susan means much more to Me than that diamond? You think she is lost, but I am taking good care of her!" And He was. What a relief that was to her. Don't ever think God is not doing what is best for your child, whom He loves more than you do. You can trust Him with that wayward child of yours, whatever the age.

Growing up, maturing and trying to make sense of the world and their place in it is a very big job. They need us to have faith in God for them.

Have you noticed that Jesus does not address sin – He addresses the heart? He is never as concerned about our sin as our prideful, stubborn hearts. Pharisees are proof of that. Judging from the outside (man's view), they looked good. *Yet*, they are the only group in the Bible that Jesus condemned (Matthew 23). He did not condemn the obvious sinners – tax collectors, prostitutes, adulterers or thieves. He goes out of His way to show that those whose hearts are for Him are those who are restored. "Your faith has made you well," He says many times (as in Mark 10:52).

Jesus told the woman at the well she was forgiven, and only afterward said, "Go and sin no more." The translation is: "You don't have to live like this anymore." Her changed behavior was *not* a condition of her release. She needed no longer be a slave to sin because He healed her *heart* (John 4). By contrast, He railed on the Pharisees *simply when they dialogued with Him!* Why? Because they were out to trick Him, because their prideful hearts were set against Him. (Matthew 3:7, for example.)

Dealing with the Sin

So how do you address your teens? If you just address their ongoing sinful behavior, you won't get very far – even though you are right and they are wrong, and you can prove it from the Bible. Even if you are successful in stopping the sin, the symptom will move elsewhere. If you press on a baggie full of icing, it's going to ooze out. Close off the opening, it will squirt out the sides. Treating the symptoms only morphs into different symptoms.

Remember that rebellion is a symptom of the heart, of a need that is not met. Kids need a *lot* of room to try on this adulthood thing as it fast approaches. They need room to stumble as they catch their stride. Much behavior is simply immaturity growing into maturity. Trying to control the behavior will not succeed like appealing to the heart. Controlling parents is often the problem, because control provokes rebellion. This is not nice to hear, but consider this: if controlling is your issue, then you can work on it and let the Lord change it in you. So that's good news!

We knew a controlling dad with three daughters, whose chastity was extremely important to him, naturally. He raised them for complete obedience, and they complied. They looked like a big happy family. But he was too controlling. He did not allow them enough decisions as they grew. Finally, the oldest girl went to a bar with some friends, found a guy and went to his house to spend the weekend. Her dad called the police, and they said, "We're sorry but since she's eighteen, there's nothing we can do." She had had enough of being denied freedom to make any choices. She later regretted her actions, but that's what controlling leads to – poor decisions motivated by rebellion. Your goal is not that they obey but that they love the Lord. You want to go for the heart, as Jesus always does.

As a family counselor, this girl's father valued his reputation to those who sought his counsel. But over-concern for our reputation can lead us to control where we should give more freedom. We are more driven than we admit by how our kids make us look.

But seeking God's agenda for the child's sake, and trying to look good as a parent, don't mix. Like oil and water. You have to choose: will I do what is best for my child as God directs me? Or will I maintain my reputation? The ironic part is, when you parent in the Lord (putting first things first), you'll get your reputation (second things) thrown in – *in the fullness of time*.

"Wisdom is justified by her children" (Matthew 11:19). That is, it takes a time to prove a course of action as wise or unwise. Children take a long time to grow and develop; we don't know the outcome except in the fullness of time. Wisdom is proved by what it produces over time.

We are wise to be teachable, to seek wise counsel, to allow our course to be corrected constantly. But it is God's counsel we must seek. To change our parenting, however subtly, to please an observer, is a diminishment of God's leading, and a disservice to our children. If you focus on the voice of the Lord, forgetting your reputation, the blessing will come back to you in the fullness of time.

I love the story of the prodigal son, a story Jesus gave us to picture how God deals with us in our rebellion (Luke 15:11-24). We can draw so many lessons from this story. The prodigal father, for instance, does not try to stop the son. He even gives him what he asked for – unthinkable, considering that by asking for his inheritance, the son is really saying, "I wish you were dead." But the father gives it to him. That may not always be what the Lord would lead us to do, but sometimes it is. The father also does not chase down the son but lets him go. Yet, when the son comes

> Our kids need to know our unconditional love for them and that we will never reject them.

back, the father sees him a long way off. So he has been watching for him. The son is coming to repent. But the father has already sent for the robe of honor and set the feast in motion *before* the son reaches him. He is ready to receive him, no questions asked, before he even hears his son's apology. That reveals God's heart of love and forgiveness for us.

Yet, I've seen parents who won't move one inch toward their struggling teen until his repentance is written in blood and he has proven he has changed. That is not God's heart for us. Repentance is part of it, certainly, but all this son did was head toward his father's house, and the dad was all over him to love him.

Our kids need to know our unconditional love for them and that we will never reject them. We want Jesus to guide our response about our teens, their friends, and today's troubled teens, not only by our words about them but by our judgments. We may know that we would accept our daughter if she came home pregnant. But she may not know that, especially when we talk about how horrible it was that the neighbor girl got pregnant. Acceptance is like an aroma that wafts over everyone. It's not that we lack judgment, but that we have compassion on those even in dire circumstances. We don't excuse or enable destructive behavior, but as the Lord increases our compassion for others, we find ourselves understanding the human plight and how people could end up where they are.

If sin is an illegitimate means to meet legitimate needs, meeting those needs will do more to bring us beyond the sin than anything else. Trees flourish not when their branches are watered but their roots.

Motivation for Behavior

What's the highest motivation for right behavior? Fear, guilt and control all motivate, but they are low motivators. What motivates to be faithful in marriage, for instance? Rob gives me a lot of freedom. He doesn't check my outgoing calls, or have me followed. So why should I remain faithful? I am faithful because I am absolutely crazy about him! That is the highest motivator. For him to check up on me would *not* increase my commitment to him; I am already motivated by the highest motivator, which is my love for him.

Now, when couples come to difficult times, a rule about being faithful can help them over a rough patch. They can cling to their commitment until their hearts come back. But it will not hold for the long haul. Aren't people having affairs day and night, people who know it's wrong, who feel guilty, who fear the consequence? Those reasons are not always sufficiently motivating to avoid an affair.

Freedom does not grant a license to sin. As *Classic Christianity* author Bob George has well said, "People are sinning quite nicely without a license." The prodigal son felt a need, for whatever reason, to try the world outside his father's house. He did, it did not satisfy, and he came back. And he was received with joy. No guilt, no fear, no reprisal. That's outlandish and makes no sense to us.

And that's the picture Jesus paints of God as our parent.

Look at how Jesus dealt with sinners: He met their need. He revealed His love for them. And over time, their pursuit of sin fell away. As new creations, the more we realize how God loves us, the more our sin falls away. Sometimes we obey because we are afraid not to. And sometimes we suffer consequences of disobedience.

But, *God longs for us to follow Him because we love Him.*

Before the Rebellion

This beautiful story of the prodigal is the answer only to the son who is *already at the point of rebellion*. He's already said, "I hate you, give me my money, I'm outta here." And the father's best choice is to let him go learn whatever he has to learn.

But Jesus is the picture of how to deal with the rebel *before he gets to full rebellion*. Jesus' every interaction (with a "pre-rebellious" person, you might say) is full of love, compassion and respect. He desires to meet the needs of the heart.

My youngest child, Hannah, adores her older sister Annie. When Hannah was eleven, Annie was away at college. Hannah and I were in the kitchen, and Hannah was being downright surly. She couldn't tell me what was wrong, so I said, "Well, you need to ask God what's wrong because you are not yourself."

She said, "Well, He won't listen! He needs to clean out His ears because He does not listen to me!"

Well! That is a terrible thing to say. I was tempted to say, "Alright, young lady, you are not to talk so disrespectfully – how can you say such a thing," etc, etc. And while I would be correct, I would immediately shut down communication. I realized that I could always say that in a minute. So I took the road less traveled and said, "Hannah, what is bothering you?" She said, "Today is Annie's birthday but she's not here and I won't see her for two months and I hate not being able to see her because she's gone!" – it all came pouring out. I hugged her and told her I understood. Within *seconds*, she apologized for what she had said about God. *Of course* she knew it wasn't true *as she said it*. And if she hadn't volunteered her apology, we would have talked about that. But by relieving her heart in talking about Annie, she was able to think more clearly instead of speaking from complete pain.

Obedience, or "right behavior," flows out of the abundant life of Christ. He shows us this in His every interaction. It's tempting to go for the behavior, but if you go for the heart, you'll get the heart and the behavior thrown in.

Look at your own life. Do you remember a time you rebelled against God? Think back on your worst period. God did not condemn you, nor get mad because He had to tell you the same thing over and over again. He did not grow impatient with you, nor was He embarrassed by you. Whether you realized it or not, He was always loving you and was always eager for you to come back.

The angels in heaven must have been shocked when Lucifer, with the world at his feet, fell so far. And many of our falls come down to the same root as Lucifer's of pride and self-service. "Jesse," a teen friend of the family, left her Christian home and got into some real trouble, with sex, drugs and other vices. Friends were shocked that Jesse, also with the world at her feet, could have fallen so far.

> Our kids are eventually going to be on their own, and we want to let the Lord equip them now.

We will avert many disasters if we first look for the unmet need driving the behavior. The dangers are out there, and sometimes the families who look most together on the outside end up with this kind of rebellion. But I believe that filling your child's need for unconditional love and acceptance at home is like immunizing them against the big dangers of a fallen world. Perhaps if Jesse had known how much her parents loved and accepted her, she would not have fallen prey to a guy who said what she longed to hear.

The heart needs must be met, and if they are not, we will do what we think will meet them. Anyone will steal food rather than die. Jesus, in His interactions with wounded people, does not zone in on the stealing; instead, He points out our hunger, and He feeds us.

Life is in Christ. Life is abiding in Him to meet the challenges that life brings us. It is not in remaining safe and unobtrusive. A boat is safe in a harbor, but that is not what a boat was designed for. Our kids are eventually going to be on their own, and we want to let the Lord equip them now. God is calling this generation to do an enormous work out there. Just look at the world. Life lived on the surface won't make it.

One women's leader said to her group, "Well, I got a can, and I thought we could put scriptures in there, and then we can pull out a verse…" She was looking at a roomful of hurting women – with broken marriages and broken families. I'm not sure that scriptures drawn from a can were going to be sufficient. We need to get to the heart. We need to cling to the Savior, who gets to the heart.

We don't need a gimmick. We don't need a quick fix. We need to let God be God and do His deep healing in us. And we need to allow Him access to our kids to equip them fully to face their generation.

Hear Them Out

If you want to know what's going on with your children, you have to be able to hear them without being shocked. Even if shock comes on you involuntarily, you will need to be able to contain it and not show your shock. Teens and women have told me about getting pregnant, having affairs, being molested, posing nude, taking drugs, trying lesbianism and attempting suicide. I know how easy it is to get to any of those places. I've done half of them, and the other half I escaped only by God's grace.

And while all these things certainly grieve my heart, none of them is outrageously shocking, considering the world we live in – with an enemy whose sole purpose is to destroy us. If you can't hear this stuff without over-reacting, they won't tell you, that's for sure. They need a *lot* of acceptance to be able to talk about such difficult topics.

I understand how kids who were molested don't tell anyone. I told my stepmother that I was uncomfortable around a certain neighbor, and she said, "Oh, Susan, he does not have any designs on you." Well, for one, she was wrong. For another, *I* then felt somehow incriminated for thinking such a thing – as if I had come up with it. But here's the most important thing: you can bet your bottom dollar I did not tell her that my brother was molesting me. Do you see what I mean? Kids will test you with something smaller, and if you freak out at that – or diminish the importance of what they are saying, or don't believe them – they won't tell you any more.

It is extremely difficult to hear that the babysitter fondled your child. But you've got to remember that as hard as it is for you to hear it, it is harder for them to tell. They are hoping that you won't lose it, and for everyone's sake, do everything you can *not* to. Listen quietly, thank them for sharing, speak only after careful consideration of your response, and do not say anything that blames them in any way. "Well, what were you doing there in the first place?" is a conversation-ender. If you *have* to know that detail, find out (without accusation) at a later time. Right now, they need to know that the two of you are okay and that they were right to tell you. "I'm so sorry that happened. Thank you for telling me – I know it was difficult. Is there anything else I need to know? You were right for telling me. I will do what I can to help you through it." These are the comments that keep communication lines open. Now is the time to reaffirm your unconditional love and acceptance. Your focus needs to be on them and not on you.

Heartwork

1. Ask the Lord to help you see your child as a new creation.
2. Remember a time you stumbled badly or rebelled. If you knew the Lord then, did you see how He addressed your heart (more than your actions)?
3. Ask the Lord to show you your teen's issues of rebellion or potential rebellion.
4. How would God have you respond to your teen's issues?
5. Ask God how He has motivated you in love.
6. Ask God how to motivate your kids in love.

• • •

meeting their needs

chapter 11
DELIGHT IN THEM (AS GOD DELIGHTS IN US)

> "The LORD your God is in your midst, A victorious warrior, He will exult over you with joy, He will be quiet in His love, He will rejoice over you with shouts of joy." Zephaniah 3:17

> "It will no longer be said to you, 'Forsaken,'
> Nor to your land will it any longer be said, 'Desolate';
> But you will be called, 'My delight is in her,'
> And your land, 'Married';
> For the LORD delights in you,
> And to Him your land will be married.
> "For as a young man marries a virgin,
> So your sons will marry you;
> And as the bridegroom rejoices over the bride,
> So your God will rejoice over you." Isaiah 62:3-5

> "The steadfast love of the Lord never ceases; his mercies never come to an end; they are new every morning; great is your faithfulness." Lamentations 3:22-23 (ESV)

God Delights in You

When we think about how God sees us, we might come up with many words. He loves us. He cares for us. He rescues us. He convicts us. He corrects us. He conforms us to the image of Christ.

But few of us would say He delights in us. Yet, He *does*. "For the Lord delights in you" (Isaiah 62:4). "He brought me forth also into a broad place; He rescued me, because He delighted in me" (Psalm 18:19). "They confronted me in the day of my calamity, but the LORD was my support. He also brought me forth into a broad place; He rescued me, because He delighted in me" (2 Samuel 22:19-21). The Lord delights in us. *He delights in us!* Even though He takes us through rough times, we are always wrapped in Him.

> I am convinced that the most important thing we can do for our children's overall sense of well-being on a daily basis is to delight in them.

God can't wait for us to wake up so He can say good morning! And He welcomes us with new mercies every morning (Lamentations 3:23). What is your response to your kids when you see them first thing in the morning? Are you delighted to see them? Do you greet them with a song in your heart and a smile on your face? Uh, me neither... but that's what we want to change! We want to parent as God parents us.

I am convinced that the most important thing we can do for our children's overall sense of well-being on a daily basis is to delight in them.

Judith Martin, aka columnist Miss Manners, in one of her adorable and witty books, made a profound observation. Her mother, as a teacher for many years, said she could tell the children who were thriving and those who were troubled by one overriding factor: how their mothers reacted to them when they picked them up from school. Some mothers' faces would light up as they saw their children. Those mothers who so delighted in their children had children who were doing well emotionally. The ones who didn't, didn't.

My family was too busy dealing with life and death and issues to delight in us kids. But God had generously provided my sister

Karin who loved me to the ends of the earth. When I walked in the kitchen in the morning, she was delighted to see me. I did not earn that! I was just me. She was a beautiful picture of God's unearned delight in me. So through all the years of torment, I always had someone who delighted in me. And though I still required a path of counseling and much healing, I knew deep down that the Lord always loved me, accepted me and approved of me (even in my rebellion). I knew He delighted in me no matter what.

My two dear friends grew up in similarly broken homes, with similarly self-consumed parents. Neither had a "Karin" – a safety net, a cheerleader in their corner, a confidant to turn to *no matter what*. And these two precious women have had a very difficult time accepting God's love and complete forgiveness – not in their heads but in their hearts. All three of us swirled around in a wind tunnel of a crazy childhood, steeped in guilt and shame, but my sister's delight tethered me – and that has made all the difference.

This is actually good news. This ability from God to delight in your children means that whatever they are going through, however bad the situation may be, your delight in them will make a huge difference. Take heart, and trust God to do the work in you and in them. Delight builds a foundation that says: "Whatever is going on, we're going to be okay. Daddy may be a drunk, Mommy may lose her temper, and we may be as poor as church mice. But, there is not something fundamentally wrong with *you* because God delights in you." Your delight in your child is a picture of God's delight in them.

If you are at an impasse, where you can't see past their actions, or your record of your child's wrongs colors your relationship – the Lord will need to work that out in you. Pray for Him to give you delight for them.

If there is too much damage to overcome right now, allow your child to spend time with someone who *does* delight in him, while God heals you.

Whatever the issue, whatever He must heal in them, your job

is to let God heal your part. If you cannot delight in them, it is because of you, not them. God delights in them, so it's not them.

Jake, whose parents finally lost their relationship with him, had an older brother who delighted in him and wanted to be with him. But because the parents did not approve of the brother's lifestyle, they would not let Jake visit him. So he lost the unconditional love he desperately needed. The irony is, he took up a similar lifestyle anyway. Of course I'm not saying that any lifestyle if fine. But Jake had already attempted suicide. He was in desperate straits, and his father was not budging. What he needed more than anything was someone who loved him, a healing balm. Someone with whom he could be himself, breathe deeply, and know he was not a loser.

"Love hopes all things, believes all things; love never fails" (1 Cor. 13:7). God calls us to love, and delight in, our children. If we don't, our first action is not to correct their behavior so that we can delight in them; our first job is to seek God and get our hearts right with Him so we can delight in them.

Pray Without Ceasing

I have had to pray for my various children at various times, in words such as these. *Dear Lord, thank You for this child of mine. Help me see any part I have in this situation that is distressing me. Thank You for being more patient with me than I am with this child! Praise You! Show me, please, where you delight in my child, as I sometimes have trouble seeing that. Show me also where you delight in me, as I sometimes have trouble seeing that as well. And please show me how I may delight in my child as you do. Amen*

Perhaps you would consider a similar prayer for you and your children.

Heartwork

1. Read these verses as if God is saying them to you (and He is): Psalm 18:16-19, Zephaniah 3:17, Isaiah 62:3-4.

2. Do you see God's delight in you? If not, ask Him to show you.
3. Is there something in your child that irritates you? Will you bring it to the Lord in prayer, asking Him to show you your part in it?
4. Ask Him to show you how He delights in your child.
5. Ask Him to show you how you may delight in your child. Pray your own prayer of delight and healing.

• • •

iii

chapter 12
ENCOURAGEMENT – THE GIFT THAT KEEPS ON GIVING

> *"If I could do it all over again – and this I would say to all young parents – make sure they know how much Jesus loves them."* Helen, youth Sunday school teacher

> *"Therefore encourage one another and build up one another, just as you also are doing."* 1 Thessalonians 5:11

> *"But encourage one another day after day, as long as it is still called today, so that none of you will be hardened by the deceitfulness of sin."* Hebrews 3:13

> *"If there is anything good – grab hold of it!"*
> Felicia, paraphrasing Philippians 4:8

A Living Eulogy

A classic life-assessment exercise is to write your eulogy. To imagine what you would want others to say about you at life's end is a great way to sort out your priorities.

Imagine for a moment that your child has died (God forbid). What would you wish with all your heart that you had told them? I would want to tell them again that I love them, that there is not a thing they could ever have done to make me love them one bit more – or one bit less. I love them completely. And Jesus loves them. He is completely satisfied with them, with the new heart He has given them, and the new creation He has made them to be –

that they are lovely, a treasure, fearfully and wonderfully made.

Loving parent, I am *not* suggesting that you tell them this in case they die. I am suggesting that you tell them this *in case they live*. For if they die, in Christ, then they will see Him face to face. They will know these things He wants them to know. They will have His full embrace, acceptance and joy. But what if they live? Then they may struggle with trying to please Him when He is already pleased. They may try to gain His acceptance when He has long since accepted them. It is a cruel trick of the enemy to tell us we are not good enough when we have become complete in Christ.

I hear time and again that full acceptance, independent of conduct, is a license to sin. *On the contrary!* Full acceptance is the greatest hedge *against* sinning because it draws on who we are in Christ. God tells us emphatically that we are accepted regardless of our behavior (Romans 8:1), because He wants us to relax in His complete acceptance, independent of our behavior.

> When we have accepted Christ as our Savior, the *real* us longs to be Christlike.

Dear friend, I have had the hardest time focusing on loving and encouraging my children when they are acting out, even though I do it very easily with my friends. Pastor and author Charles Swindoll said that we usually interact with the flesh in people and let the Christ in them be. But the opposite is required. Interact with the Christ in them and let the flesh be.

Our redeemed heart longs for righteousness. When we have accepted Christ as our Savior, the real us longs to be Christlike. We don't long to sin. And when we do sin, for a season, God sorts it out. Telling us not to sin does not stop our sin. Reconfirming the Christ in us will lead us back to repentance. (It's God's kindness that leads us to repentance.)

Let's walk through a few examples together. Imagine going to a job day after day, in which your boss vigorously points out your shortcomings. He does not notice your achievements, of course, but will tell you about your mistakes. Would you be inspired to work harder to please this boss? Or would you feel weighed down, perhaps begin wishing for another job?

Or, imagine that your spouse is generally not pleased with you. Whatever you do with the kids, at home, you can't seem to win. Are you inspired to try to do better? Or do you begin to wonder how you can live this way?

Contrast that to a boss or spouse who is constantly pleased with what you do. "Great job on those reports... This is just what I need... I couldn't do this job without you." You would do absolutely anything for him! When we are truly appreciated in our job, we only strive to do more. "What else can I do for you? Take your clothes to the cleaners? Absolutely! Work hard to finish this for you? Of course!"

Please understand, I am not trying to minimize the terribly painful situation people find themselves in – I'm saying that when we are encouraged, we rise; when discouraged, we shrink. When encouraged, courage is put into us; when discouraged, courage is taken out of us.

Believe me, if I seem to be pointing a finger at you, it means I've got four pointed back at me. I find myself well aware of my children's mistakes and sometimes have to make a conscious effort to compliment or encourage them. I have improved only because I have fervently sought the Lord for help.

We can require encouragement in our homes. Some of our kids have been fond of correcting their siblings and telling them where they were wrong or what they should do. Our maxim became: "Your job is to encourage your siblings, not to correct them... Your job is to encourage your siblings, not to correct them... Your job is to encourage your siblings, not to correct them."

Similarly, we had a house rule: no name-calling. God does not call us names, except terms of endearment – like "beloved." (I like that one!) If family members are allowed to call each other names, the home ceases to be the safe place of respite that we all need. Even calling someone "the smart one" or "the skinny one" puts them in a box – and places the other siblings out of that box by comparison. That becomes their identity, the very thing God seeks to break in us.

What you focus on will increase. If you can encourage your kids where you see their attempts to do well, they will increase. Ask the Lord where your kids are doing well, and genuinely encourage them there.

At one point, one of my children was very attentive to correcting the other kids. I pointed this out and said to stop. But only when I focused on this child, increasing random hugs, enjoying his presence, relaxing and delighting in him, did the other behavior decrease. This child needed more attention, got it, and the other "illegitimate" means decreased.

Heartwork

1. If you are willing, write your own eulogy – ways you would want people to remember you.
2. Ask the Lord to encourage you, how He sees you and what He is doing in you. Listen to Him and believe what He says. You don't have to trust yourself to hear Him as much as trust Him to speak to you.
3. If you had only one more chance to talk to your child, what would you want to say? What do you love about him? Think of as many ways to encourage your child as possible.
4. Sit down with your child and tell him all that you appreciate about him. Be sincere and thorough. Many will respond like a parched plant to water. Whether or not you get a positive reaction, trust the Lord to work it in him for good.
5. Have you found yourself condemning your child? Ask the Lord to show you the child through His eyes and to speak encouragement through you.
6. Do your children need to increase their encouragement for each other? Will you make a conscious effort to train them in (and model) encouragement of everyone in the family?

7. Ask the Lord if there are other areas (like name-calling and negative humor) you can change to make the home a safe haven.

• • •

chapter 13
RESPECT VERSUS SHAME

> *"Let me not be put to shame, O LORD, for
> I call upon You." Psalm 31:17*

> *"An excellent wife is the crown of her husband, but she who
> shames him is like rottenness in his bones." Proverbs 12:4*

> *"Let the words of my mouth and the meditation of my heart be acceptable in Your sight, O LORD, my rock and my Redeemer." Psalm 19:14*

> *"R-E-S-P-E-C-T. Find out what it means to me." R-E-S-P-E-C-T, sung by Aretha Franklin*

I respect my husband. I respect my friends. I respect my hairdresser, the mailman and grocery sacker. The ones I have trouble respecting are my children. Yes, I love them, I am proud of them, and I think they've done a terrific job growing up. I couldn't ask for another thing, and I don't wish they were any different. I really don't.

> I view them as an inconvenience too often
> and as a gift from God too seldom.

What I mean is that on a daily basis, when I'm asking them to empty the dishwasher, or brush their teeth, or to play a board game with me, I don't speak respectfully. This is not always true, of course, and not always obvious. It is tempting to say that it is because of their behavior that I speak disrespectfully, but it's not. It is because I don't value them as I say I do. I view them as an inconvenience too often and as a gift from God too seldom. I would not let anyone *else* speak to them the way I sometimes speak to them. I hope their spouses speak with more respect than I often do.

My husband had been pointing this out to me, lovingly – and rightfully. And I knew he was correct. But I did not seem to be able to change my way of interacting.

> ...the mother's harshness made the children cringe, and finally to stop listening.

Then I was visiting some friends out of state – people I dearly love and admire and treat as family. I had not seen them in ages, and I noticed that their children bickered with each other – a constant nattering that gets under the skin. Then I noticed that the mother spoke to them in the same harassed voice: *Why did you do that? Don't you know better than to leave this out? If you had not played so roughly, this wouldn't have broken.* Of course children need to be taught. But the mother's harshness made the children cringe, and finally to stop listening.

I was undone. I saw what Rob had been trying to tell me for a long time: it was not my words of correction but my unpleasant way of saying them that was driving the kids up the wall. I was not kind to them the way I am to others. Sometimes I am kind of course, but often I am downright rude. It was not until I saw my friend's interaction with her children that I saw my own unlovely, and unloving tone with my children.

Too often I have made my children feel small because of their youth, childish inabilities, or immaturity. How many mistakes did I make in my youth, with my carelessness or immaturity? I am thankful not to be answering for it still. Sometimes I recall my youthful mistakes and flush with embarrassment. Do you ever feel that way? I am not talking about gross, overt sins; I'm talking about neglecting to appreciate someone, or taking the best for myself, or being a know-it-all. These don't usually make the Richter scale like adultery or murder. But they are insidious for their commonness.

There's a word for this embarrassment long after the fact: shame. Shame fills us with regret and embarrassment over transgressions long forgotten by everyone else. The thing we need to know about our new and amazing covenant with God is – He does not shame us. Even in our grossest sins, He does not shame us.

Imagine being caught in bed with a man not your husband. Not only caught but dragged into the open public square. Not only dragged out but having your sin told to the pastor. And then they ask him what should be done to you. Can you simply imagine the shame? But how did Jesus respond in this situation? He turned on the men who brought her. He treated her with respect. Oh, the sheer joy of knowing that we need not be ashamed. He took away not only our sin but our *shame*. Joy. Peace that passes understanding.

Oh, Lord, speak through me to my children, words of life, words of love. Help me correct them, yes, but sweetly, lovingly, patiently – as You correct me.

God does convict me. When I begin to judge someone for an irritating habit, the Lord is faithful to remind me of my own irritating habit! Isn't that faithful of Him? But it is not shame. It is not humiliation, defeat, and the weight of my complete inadequacy. It is conviction which brings with it hope.

> When a child is sexually abused, that is only the beginning of the problem. The bigger part comes from the years that follow as the shame cements itself in the heart.

This is a tough topic. I was awhile in understanding the concept of shame, understanding the full weight of it and how predisposed we are to shaming others and ourselves. If you let the Lord shed light, you will begin to see shame everywhere. It does not come from God.

A sweet teenager was staying us, and I asked her to call everyone to dinner. My younger son did not come immediately. She said cheerfully to me in his hearing: "Mrs. Cottrell, doesn't it make you sad when people don't come to dinner after you worked so hard to make it?" This study of shame was fresh on my heart!

I said pleasantly, "No, I don't shame my kids into coming to dinner! They need to come because they were called, not because it will make me sad." She looked stunned; her parents shamed their kids often, which was part of the breakdown that had brought her to live with us.

If this is a new concept, it will not immediately make complete sense. But as you seek the Lord about it, He will reveal what He wants you to see.

Heartwork

1. Think back on moments you were embarrassed. Can you still feel it now? Can you feel the "aargh," wishing you could change the moment?
2. Can you identify feelings of shame – inadequacy, unworthiness, sorrow? Shame usually accompanies sexual sin (for both perpetrator and victim); family, marital or financial problems; and other problems that you may or may not have enabled. Ask the Lord to help you see the shame you carry.
3. If you have identified those feelings, ask the Lord to heal you. Remember that He does not shame us – that is the enemy's doing. He does not even condemn us. "There is therefore now no condemnation for those who are in Christ Jesus" (Romans 12:1).
4. Ask the Lord if you have shamed your children. You do not need to take on shame for it, but you may need to grieve.

Take the time you need with this.
5. Ask the Lord how to make amends. You may need to ask Him to change the way you interact with them, and you may need to ask their forgiveness.
6. Thank Jesus for dying on the cross not only for our sin but also for our shame.
7. Praise Him!

• • •

chapter 14
GUIDE THEM (AS GOD GUIDES)

"The world is a looking-glass, and gives back to every man the reflection of his own face. Frown at it, and it will in turn look sourly upon you; laugh at it and with it, and it is a jolly kind companion; and so let all young persons take their choice." Unknown

"Children of dysfunctional families develop roles to survive in an emotionally dangerous environment."
Tim Sledge, Making Peace with Your Past

"We are immigrants to the computer age; our kids are natives." Rob Whitaker, comparing parents' and kids' facility with technology.

Our kids have access to cell phones, texting, the Internet, and lots of interactions with real people apart from us. While we parents spent time as teenagers talking to one person on the phone, they are talking to twenty people on Facebook! We have a great opportunity to coach them in wisdom to interact with this broad range of communication. By teaching them discernment – as Jesus taught His disciples – we equip our children in the choices they will make choices for themselves. Remember, our goal is to wean them from us and onto the Lord. The Eighteen-Year Master Plan is their complete dependence on Him – their fount of ongoing wisdom.

If you skip over discipling them, and instead try to intercept everything, be in on everything, read emails, phone calls, and deny access to cell phones and the Internet, the likely result will be anarchy. Be prepared for an explosion of everything that was not allowed the moment the teen/young adult does gain access. It is far better to give access and monitor as you go, while training in dangers and wise use.

> Meanwhile, the years that could have been spent as partners, seeking to gain victory, were lost in attempts at control.

A friend of my son Chris was going to spend the night with us. His mother asked if there was a TV in the house – there was. She said, "Well, is there any way to lock it up because if he can get access to it, he'll watch it all night." I said, "Really?" This was a young man of fifteen – not a rebel, no special needs – and his parents had to bar him physically from watching TV all night. She later confided that they were afraid he would watch pornography because he had watched it before. Okay, now this is very serious stuff and I want to be sure you understand my heart here. Pornography is extremely damaging to men, and to women. But the question is: how are you going to deal with it? This family restricted their son in every way possible from access. But let me tell you something. The son will eventually move out. And those parents won't be able to monitor him then. Meanwhile, the years that could have been spent as partners, seeking to gain victory, were lost in attempts at control.

Contrast that to another family whose son similarly began looking at pornography on the web. (I was shocked when I realized that some ninety percent of men struggle with this issue.) That father embraced the son and said, "We'll work through this." He sought the son's heart on whether he saw that it was a problem. It actually took some conversing for the son finally to see why pornography was harmful. They became a team, both of them committed to helping him stop. The father did not remove the Internet, but checked to see whether the son had used it. The parents did not shame him, but took it as a battle to be fought together that the enemy had waged.

Now here's the most telling thing about this. The father of the first son, the one who tried to control access, was later revealed to have a serious addiction to porn. It is telling because he did not know how to end it, did not end it in himself, and perhaps didn't really want to end it. So when it occurred with his son, his only idea was to control. The second father, who came alongside his son, did not have a struggle with porn. Interesting, isn't it?

Surely we want to block cable channels when there are younger children in the house – no need to be foolhardy. But we have to be forward-thinking, to train them toward maturity. We can police them while they are younger, and increase their freedoms as they grow. If you try to parent by control, you override their internal controls, which creates big problems.

If you grew up in a dysfunctional home – and just about who didn't? – *please* allow someone to help you. There is no shame in not knowing how to do these things. Who in the world does? The shame is in *not* humbling yourself so that God can teach you.

We know a woman whose father was so controlling that she shot her husband rather than telling her father she needed a divorce. Can you imagine feeling so trapped as to kill your husband rather than admit you need a divorce? This is just one story I happen to know about – how many are out there?

When Rob and I first went through counseling, we both had course corrections to make. At one point, the counselor asked me a question, and I knew the answer was unflattering to us. I glanced at Rob. I love him and respect him and did not want to hurt him. You know what he did? He said, "Go ahead. Say whatever you need to say." He knew the only way to health and restoration was to address whatever it was. Bless his heart. I don't even remember the item, which doesn't matter now. But I will always remember that he tenderly encouraged me to speak, because restoring health to our family was more important to him than saving face.

Admit you need help and let someone help you. I have sought a lot of help over the years! A *lot*. I wouldn't go back for anything.

> Dysfunction is not defined as *having* problems; dysfunction is that we do not *admit* our problems.

The only difference I see between growing into a healthy family or remaining in our dysfunction is our willingness to say: *Okay, Lord, I surrender. I can't do it. You are the only One who can heal this problem.*

One terribly abusive father cannot understand how his adult kids want nothing to do with him. He said to his daughter: "What did I do that was so terrible, that all my kids hate me?" But the moment she began to tell him, just a bit, he turned it around on her. He doesn't want to know. He wants them to say, "Everything was fine, Dad, really." By that point, honestly, it's tough to bring restoration. The adult child is doing all he can to recover himself; he can't be fixing Dad.

But we won't go down that path. As painful as it is, when something comes up, let's agree that we will honestly seek the Lord and let Him address it – even if it means a major overhaul – because it will be worth whatever He has to lead us through. He is trustworthy and highly qualified!

Dysfunction is not defined as having problems; dysfunction is that we do not admit our problems. How many families have issues? One hundred out of one hundred. How many families have times they are glad no one was videotaping life in their house? Ninety-nine out of one hundred! When my kids were little and I would lose my temper, I thanked God no one else was watching. But the freedom comes in being able to admit our problems – and in that, admit our need for the Lord.

In recent senate hearings about the problems of steroid use in professional sports, one ballplayer would not admit to steroid use, though there were many testimonies of his using it. A commentator said: "How are we going to get the neighborhood addict to admit his problem when these highly visible players won't admit theirs?" Admission is half the solution.

When sexual abuse is revealed early, complete healing is practically assured; it is the secrecy (and the shame that piles on top of that) that makes it so damaging. That's why satan is committed to darkness and lies. As the father of lies, satan thrives in darkness, but God is truth and light.

Counselors say, "You are only as sick as your secrets." It is not the thing itself that makes us sick but the need to hide it, which changes it into something far worse than the thing itself. We all have issues – it is the healthy of us who realize it – and we *all* need a Savior.

Years ago, Rob and I were on a transatlantic ocean-liner in late November, and the seas were stormy the whole trip. We rocked and rolled, and a piano rolled off the stage and broke. Items had to be battened down. I looked out across the ocean and saw another ocean-liner. Do you know that ocean-liner looked completely calm? I couldn't see any rocking. But I knew that ship was on the same sea and had to be moving as much as we were – we just couldn't see it.

It's true in our lives. While our own ship is rocking wildly, we look at everyone around us, certain they don't have problems, or certainly not as bad as ours, and we put on a good face.

But if we can seek God, and reach out to someone else, and be transparent, we will find that others have similar problems. We don't need to be ashamed, but we can get the help we need, however God wants to provide it.

Heartwork

1. What issues have your children been facing? Have you tried to control those issues? How has it worked?
2. Do your teens desire more freedom? (You may need to ask them.) What is the Lord telling you about that?
3. Will you admit to the problems in your family? Do you see the need to surrender your problems to Him?
4. Ask Him where you need outside help; ask Him where to find that help.

5. "But seek first His kingdom and His righteousness, and all these things [your needs] will be added to you" Matthew 6:33. Ask the Lord what you have been seeking first ahead of Him. Ask Him to help you seek Him first.

• • •

chapter 15
GIRLS, GUYS AND SEXUAL IDENTITY

"Above all else, guard your heart, for it is the wellspring of life." Proverbs 4:23

"I have loved you with an everlasting love." Jeremiah 31:3

"You have stolen my heart, my sister, my bride, you have stolen my heart with one glance of your eyes." Song of Solomon 4:9

Girls and Guys

Perhaps the greatest potential for health or wounding, other than how we portray God to our children, is how we convey sexual identity, along with sexuality. My friend joked that she is saving *not* for her children's college fund but for their therapy fund. We parents long to spare our children the mound of problems inflicted on us. But the area of sexual identity and sexuality is so volatile, it seems impossible not to pass on our baggage.

Complete treatments have been done on this subject, and I can't do that here. But we will accomplish much if we simply begin to fill our children's deep need to be affirmed in their sexual identity.

Guys

Boys need to hear, regularly and authentically, that they have what it takes to be a man. *Wild at Heart* by John Eldredge taught me how vulnerable men are and how vital it is that they see their own abilities as men. Whether your son is an athlete, a pianist, a writer or anything else, he needs constant affirmation that God has equipped him fully as a man, and God will faithfully complete the good work He began in him (Philippians 1:6). Dads especially need to engage with their sons – affirming, including and accepting them as the person God designed them to be.

Mom's job is to let their boys grow up, let them separate, encourage them to take risks and trust them to become men. Tell them you know they can do it. Hold the crown above their head and let them grow into it.

I failed at this when my family was at a rock-climbing wall at the fair. Our David, barely four, wanted to climb. I immediately decided $5 was too much to pay for him to climb two feet and then quit. I foolishly told Rob that Dave was too little and could not do it. He said, "I can do it, Mom." Rob paid the money and David did climb – all the way to the top. And when he got down, he said, "See Mom? I knew I could do it." Risking my son's view of his manhood is not worth saving $5.

Not only do our boys need to believe they have what it takes to be men and to succeed, they also need to understand that their job is to love and protect the women in their lives – mothers, wives, sisters, daughters. They need to esteem girls, encourage them, treat them with dignity, and not use them for their own pleasure. If boys would treat the girls in their lives as they hope their future wives are being treated, what a sweet impact that would make in our culture.

One day, a boy came into our church carrying a frog. I went on high alert, feeling as I do about frogs. My husband admired the frog, as any boy deserves his frog to be admired; then he said, "Don't get that frog near my wife." He said it with intent, calmly and firmly. The boy did not come near me. Men, that kind of protection will win your wife's heart like you can't believe. It shows such love for her, will reap dividends you cannot imagine and will earn her undying loyalty to you. We want to train our boys to be the protector, not the perpetrator!

Our church bulletin listed this class: "Wives, Learn to Love Your Husbands." My husband whispered to me, "What about, 'Husbands, Learn to Love Your Wives'?" Our churches do a thorough job of teaching women to submit, a touchy subject these days. But far fewer men are taught to love their wives as Christ loved the church. Christ laid down His life for the church. Few men physically die for their family, but all are asked to lay down their life daily, which Christ demonstrated as the very essence of servant leadership. We will bless our sons and their families forever if we pass on to them servant leadership.

Paul rightly echoed Christ as a champion of women in the ancient world, though without context, we can wrongly conclude the opposite. (His instruction of Timothy, for instance, was to address specific problems in the church, such as rampant goddess worship but without context, it sounds like subjugation of women.) Short of an adequate background study, perhaps we can come much nearer the heart of Christ's teaching simply by observing how He treated women with love, honor and respect, in a day when women were treated as property. Fathers and sons can read those stories together – Luke 7:36-50, John 4:1-26, John 8:3-12, and even John 19:25-27, when in His dying moments, Jesus assures that His mother will be cared for without Him. These are remarable stories of love and healing. No wonder every woman who met Jesus in Person was transformed.

> If we will teach our sons their job of loving and protecting women, our world will be a safer, sweeter place.

Girls

Girls need to be affirmed that they are lovely, they are Daddy's little darlings, and they are indeed growing into lovely women. God built this need into girls, and those whose daddies do not adore them will soon find someone who will.

Many fathers mistakenly believe that if they deny this need, they will avoid raising a girl who thinks too highly of herself. On the contrary, they will raise a girl who is desperate to prove her desirability.

Consider this: I always loved pizza. I would request it as often as I could have it. It was never too much. Then in college, I worked in a pizza place. I got to eat pizza on every shift and take extra pizza home. I had as much pizza as I could hold. My desire for pizza was so satisfied that I completely lost my taste for it. It took a good ten years before I even would eat pizza and another ten before I ever actually desired one.

Do you see what I'm saying? To deny a heart need is to multiply it dramatically. Conversely, even the most gaping need will shrink as we fill it. It is possible to make sure our children know they are loved, so that they can put off finding that special someone for a long, long time. If this need is not filled, even a twelve-year-old may seek to fill it in the worst possible way. Many relationship problems come from people trying to prove they are worthy of love and respect. To pour that love and respect into them in their very own home will prevent many of those heart-wrenching problems.

We have endeavored to make sure our own girls know they are loved, lovely, and worthy. They also see their daddy treat me with honor and respect. We do not want them thinking the world revolves around them. We also do not want to teach them the world revolves around their husband. Strict churches that teach

> Brothers, friends, classmates – all can benefit by a girl's loving encouragement and kindness.

wives submission, without teaching husbands to love their wives as their own bodies, set women up to be controlled and abused. Christ set the ancient world on its ear when He treated women with dignity and tenderness. It is still our call.

Not only do our girls need a safe place to become who they were meant to be, but they also need to be a safe place for the young men in their lives to unfold as men. Guys can get messed up simply trying to impress a girl! Countless stories show the guy walking into a pole as he was trying to impress a girl. It's built in. Girls can be helpful simply by encouraging and not emasculating them. Brothers, friends, classmates – all can benefit by a girl's loving encouragement and kindness.

Girls have a wide range of options available to them, in service, in family, in career. Moms have great opportunity to strengthen their daughter's hearts desire. To serve them well, we need to teach them to love the Lord completely, to allow Him to open into their giftings and use them, not to fit into a mold. God is far too creative and loving and wonderful to fit all of women's offerings into one mold. We must hear from Him for each individual daughter or son.

Guys and Girls Together

It is said that we marry our mom or dad, and when I have wondered at someone's choice of boyfriend, fiancé or spouse, the answer often is simply to look at the parent. A beautiful girl's over-controlling boyfriend is usually not far off from her father. A young man whose fiancé is unpleasable usually has a similar mother. Without God's healing, this scenario plays itself out in countless love relationships.

And so, by letting God transform our own marriages, we will do more for our children than any marriage tidbits we might teach them. It comes down to simple love and respect. Showing love and respect for each other instills those values in our children. Dad teaches his son how to treat a wife by how he treats Mom, and Mom teaches her daughter how to interact with a husband by how she treats Dad.

But in addition, Dad teaches his daughter what to expect from her husband and Mom teaches her son what to expect in a wife.

That is, when Dad treats his wife lovingly – speaking kindly, holding doors open, caring for her heart – he teaches his daughters that this is not too much to expect of a man worthy of her. When Mom respects her husband – speaking well of him, believing in him, understanding the weight on his shoulders – she teaches her son that he deserves to be treated with respect by his wife. Of course the opposite is true too, as we teach negative as well as positives.

A whole marriage comes from two whole people. We have enormous opportunity to model that to our children *as God creates wholeness in us*. Raising your sons and daughters to be whole, in the Lord, will best prepare them for a satisfying marriage.

Heartwork

1. Do your sons know they have what it takes to be men? Do you see ways in which you need to encourage them as men?
2. How can you hold the crown above their heads and let them grow into it? Do you need to affirm them?
3. How would God lead you to teach your sons to protect, serve and defend the women in their lives?
4. Do your girls know they are lovely? Are they Daddy's little darlings?
5. How would God have you fill that heart-need to be treasured?
6. How can you love your girls to overflowing?
7. Ask God for a vision of your children as the men and women He designed them to be. Ask Him to show you how He sees them, and how you can nurture them that direction.

• • •

chapter 16
DATING AND SEXUALITY

"If you're going out with a guy, you have to know your boundaries before you get in the truck!" A Texas teenager at Sunday school

"If you tell me how far is too far in my dating relationship, I don't need God anymore! It's giving me a formula to replace a relationship." Steve Volie, Bodensehoff Bible School

"Dating today is like playing Russian Roulette." A homeschool mom

Dating

How do we manage the question of dating? In a day when even third-graders are paired off, it is a definite upstream swim to remain "unattached." Yet, we parents see the casualties out there and know the risks, as we have lived through them.

Let me tell you, we need Jesus to walk through this with us.

If we could have our way, many Christian parents would say it's wise not to date until the late teens, or until ready for marriage. We see serial dating as training for divorce (by giving up and moving on). Other parents will consider only courtship. And some consider it harmless – even adorable – for their young teen or even gradeschooler to have a boyfriend or girlfriend.

Twenty parents will come up with at least fifteen answers on best rules for relationship! So what do we do?

First, let us turn from the tree of knowledge and toward the tree of life. We have to seek out Jesus for specific leading – different leading for different children in the same family. No one answer works for every child or for every family.

> If a formula could make this work, that would be the law; we could do it ourselves without need of a Savior.

Look at courtship, for instance. It sounds great on paper, and many times it works well. I know some young couples court and end up happily married. But it does not always work out; sometimes it merely turns a girl over from a controlling father to a controlling husband, without her feet ever touching the ground. One girl from a legalistic family developed a long-distance courtship, and then married. But the husband turned out to be a controller who denied his wife permission even to see her parents. She is miserable. The successful scenarios came from more than just deciding on "courtship."

Is courtship on the good or bad list? Neither. (Trick question.) If we do courtship according to the tree of life, it works; if we do it according to the tree of knowledge, it fails. *This is true of anything*.

I have seen a wide variety of approaches; each one has worked in some families and not worked in others. To complicate matters here, some couples have done everything right and end up in miserable relationships. Others do everything wrong and end up in lifelong happiness. The truth is that each story is unique and there is no foolproof formula. We can look at guidelines, but there is no guarantee. If a formula could make this work, that would be the law; we could do it ourselves without need of a Savior. These relationships, like everything else, come down to heart-connected dependence on Jesus.

Seeking Him is the bottom line. He will guide you through this minefield like nothing else can. We have to be willing to hear Him (both parent and child) – not like my son who always got the Lord's okay to buy the Lego set! If you and your child are at different places, sometimes He will move the child, and sometimes

He will move you.

Your teens need you to partner with them on this. I'm not saying you cannot set the rules, but your kids must own the rules. Some families have successfully said, "No dating until sixteen." Others with the same rule have found their teens sneaking around or rebelling. While family dynamics vary widely, the difference between compliance and rebellion seems to be whether the whether the teen ultimately owns the rules. Parents who respect, dialogue with and *listen* to the teen's heart in this decision-making process become partners with them, and have far better success than those who lay down the rules.

Both submitting to the Lord and respecting your teen are about eating from the tree of life. Both are about relationship over the list. And both essentially boil down to Jesus' great command, to love God and love your neighbor (in this case, your teen).

Rules can be helpful – but only rules the teen gets behind. As a teen, I set rules for myself (for lack of adult guidance), and they kept me from the heat of the moment more than once. Similarly, rules in a marriage can keep us from heading down a road we never meant to head down (such as not being alone with someone of the opposite gender, a rule many ministry leaders have set for themselves). But the rule is only a helper for resolve already made; it can easily give way when the desire gets too great. The heart has to be in it, and the teen has to own it.

Our girls have purity rings, presented to them specially by Rob and me. But this was after we had discussed it, they made the commitment, and they asked for the rings. It is only a reminder of a heart commitment they already owned.

Boys can have a similar ceremony ushering them into manhood, as our son did upon turning thirteen. Several men from our church joined Rob and our son for a "knighting ceremony" during which they told our son of the wonderful qualities they saw in him, how they had seen him grow since they knew him, and gave him hope for the future.

The idea is to know our kids, respect them as God made them, and nurture them to unfold in God's hand.

A Case Study

One experience showed us the importance of letting God lead and guide, without our own standards getting in the way. Our daughter, at thirteen, asked us if she could date someone she had met through school. We said no. She wanted to comply, and she did comply. But it was very hard for her. Soon she appealed to us in tears, saying she had prayed about it, and she felt that God was saying that he was worth a second look. We were at an impasse. We respected her prayer, her own leading of the Lord.

(Remember, even if a particular item appears self-serving, like, "God said I could date!" we must respect that. We do not have to agree; we can say that we need Him to confirm it to us as well. But to dismiss their word from Him undermines their own desire to seek Him for themselves – as in, why bother if they're going to reject it anyway? Better to act on hearing Him wrongly and learn from *that*, provided the stakes are not too dangerous or irreversible.)

Rob and I reconvened and prayed again. Then Rob called her in and asked her what it meant to date. (After all, they were not going anywhere; they saw each other only at school.) She said, "It means that you have special feelings for each other, you eat lunch together, you might hold hands." We confirmed that nothing else would be involved. Then Rob said, "If that's all it means, you are allowed to date him." She threw her arms around him, overjoyed. "If anything else happens, then that's a different question!" I added as she skipped out of the room.

She kept to those rules, and we had the young man over for dinner and for a family outing.

Within a month, she came to us in tears saying she was going to have to break up with him. She said he does not love the Lord the way she thought, and God did not want her to date him anymore. In a heart-wrenching phone call, she broke up with him.

Then she came and climbed in her daddy's lap and cried. Our only words were of consolation and comfort. (Not a word about her having misheard, us being right or any of that, which would have destroyed everything *God* was doing in her.) She had experienced something unique, with no collateral damage, which God used to guide her. Even talking about it a few years later, she told me she was glad for the experience and all God taught her through it.

I realize that many sincere Christians will disagree with our approach. They would say we should have stayed with our no. But we sought the Lord sincerely and listened to Him. And I think we all benefited from the "yes" in ways we could not have antici-

> I feel like His favorite child...And so, I will do anything for Him.

pated. We honored her heart for the Lord, and she came through unharmed but wiser. I also believe that saying no would have stirred up dissonance in her heart, and put unnecessary distance between us. But I say that only because I trust that God guided us at every turn.

On the other hand is my girlfriend whose daughter also came to her about dating someone from school. The family rule is no dating before sixteen, and over sixteen, it is on a case-by-case basis. The parents talked at length with her; they encouraged her to write down what qualities she was drawn to in this guy for future reference in a mate; and ultimately, their "no" stood. A few years later, the girl thanked them for standing firm. The key is that each child is different and should be treated as such. There is no rule here that works for everybody – except, "Seek the Lord."

God is amazingly personal in His relationships with us. It is one of my favorite traits about Him! I feel like His favorite child. Who wouldn't love that? And so, I will do anything for Him.

Case Study Two

"Jason" at fourteen was not allowed to date. (Again, this dating meant hanging out at school – they didn't actually go anywhere.) He knew the rule but he did it anyway, lying about it. His parents learned of this "accidentally." (Always pray your children will get caught!) And so they had a talk. Dad explained that now they had two problems: dating and – far more damaging – *lying*. Dad explained that his idea of parenting was to allow as much freedom as the child could handle while the child grew increasingly dependent on Jesus. He believed this produced the most responsible, Christ-centered adult. The son's part was to grow in the Lord. Dad recounted several ways in which the son had grown. And the son added a few ways that he saw. Dad asked if his son liked the freedom he had been given, and the son answered yes.

Then Dad pointed out the problem: if Jason would not respect his parents' authority and trust them even when he didn't agree, then that would mean Jason had too much freedom, and they would necessarily have to restrict it. Dad said: "Jason, you will either follow after the Lord with all your heart, or you will follow after yourself, with all your heart. That is what Joshua meant when he said, 'Choose for yourselves today whom you will serve… but as for me and my house, we will serve the Lord' [Joshua 24:15]. Jason, I want you to spend some time with the Lord and talk to Him about who you want to serve. Either choice will result in certain consequences. You decide what you're going to do, and then Mom and I will decide what we're going to do."

The beauty is that Jason's dad treated him with respect and freedom to choose God for himself. Jason was given grace to make mistakes and rectify them. He did choose the Lord for himself. And though Dad took his phone away briefly (as a taste of things to come down the road of restricted freedom), he stood ready to restore completely and start from a clean slate. Remember that is what the prodigal father did with his son, in that lovely picture of how God is with us. We can follow up, watch them, and pray for God to reveal the issues. And we stand ready to forgive and start from a clean slate.

Case Study Three

"Mike" loved the Lord. Mike also discovered pornography on the Internet. He spent six months using pornography before he realized how damaging it was to him and attempted to quit. He had been pure with the few girls he dated in high school, but became sexually active after discovering porn. When his father discovered it (by checking the son's Internet history), he had a talk with Mike. Mike agreed he needed help, and together they worked through it. He overcame his "addiction" and agreed to set up a filter that would report to his dad all sites visited, so his dad could hold him accountable.

It was a struggle, but through it he came clean. He voluntarily continued his accountability through college, for his own benefit. We must be realistic in seeing that a problem area usually takes time to change. I did not stop yelling the first time I realized how harmful it was. The process usually includes making the same mistake many times. But, it is necessary to do as Jason's dad did and as the prodigal father did, and wipe the slate clean for a fresh start. That's what it means to hold no record of wrongs. Again, each case is unique, each child is unique, and God will lead uniquely, according to His unfathomable wisdom. *His* plan will restore life.

Eye on the Goal

The mistake I see most often is living from the rulebook, without listening to the unique child. Not all children are the same any more than all adults are the same.

What is the long-term goal here? It is healthy male-female relationships, healthy marriages – or healthy singleness, if that is God's call. This includes healthy sexuality. All of this comes through hearing the Lord with the teen as he continues to develop the ability to hear Him for himself.

Sexuality

The many swimming pools here in Phoenix pose a constant danger of drowning, and we have pool enclosure laws, media awareness campaigns and tiny-tot swim lessons. What no one has proposed is a law to remove all swimming pools. Pools provide such fun and cooling refreshment during our scorching summers that we would rather beef up water safety than give up pools.

Now, let's talk about sex. Sex provides fun and refreshment, intimacy and bonding. God designed it before the fall as an expression of intimacy between a man and a woman, as a picture of our intimacy with Him. Sex is arguably one of His most brilliant ideas. Sex is good, despite the dangers associated with it.

The trouble is that our mortal enemy does everything possible to ruin sex. Chagrined that he did not think of this brilliant idea himself, he works feverishly to distort it into something it is not.

Here are two things I see the enemy doing to sex: put it where it shouldn't be, and kill it where it should be. He entices singles to sleep together and spouses to have affairs. Date rape on college campuses is epidemic and chastity is ridiculed. Pornography is the scourge of men and boys at all levels. And untold innocents have been severely wounded by abuse and molestation.

> As damaging as it is to operate under the law once we have come to God under grace, it is damaging to view sex as a dirty thing once we have become one in marriage.

Conversely, the enemy attacks sex within marriage, just as happy to stop sex between spouses as to stir it up between non-spouses. Jokes abound about how good sex was – until they got married. While plenty of married couples enjoy the wonderful gift of sex God offers, countless couples do not. I have heard from many Christian women who do not have sex in their own marriage. God has given Christian couples the gift of sex, and the enemy has done his best to destroy it.

Here is why I'm saying all this: sexuality is an area rife for conveying our own dysfunction to our children. Most Christian parents do an outstanding job of instilling the dangers of sex into their teens. But most of them forget to say: "Oh, this only applies until you're married! Once you're married, you are free to enjoy it, it will be great, and it will help bond you to your spouse." As damaging as it is to operate under the law once we have come to God under grace, it is damaging to view sex as a dirty thing once we have become one in marriage. To paraphrase Acts 10:15: "What God has designed beautifully, let no man call unclean."

Let us go back to the swimming pool analogy. Imagine a family whose child drowned in their backyard pool. As much fun as other families have swimming in the summer, that family would not likely view swimming in any fun way again. Surely healing is needed, however long and painful the road to it. But they might not be the best ones to ask whether you should put a pool in your yard.

Similarly, the lasting impact of sexual abuse and legalistic, unhealthy childhoods is not easily rectified. We subconsciously pass on our own unhealthy sexual imprint to our beloved children. I encourage the wounded to seek healing and to seek appropriate ways to prepare their children for healthy sexuality.

You want to observe the old doctor's oath: "First, do no harm." Though it is impossible not to imprint your children in some way with your own feelings about sexuality, if you seek help with it, perhaps from a trusted family member, friend or pastor, you may be able to instill in them a more healthy view of sexuality. This area is important enough to do whatever is necessary to restore to them what the enemy has done his best to steal.

Heartwork

1. Where do you and your teens stand right now with dating?
2. Ask the Lord for vision as to what their needs are individu

ally, and what kind of path He has for them individually. Ask the Lord how He would have you guide your kids through this challenging area.
3. Ask the Lord where you have unhealthy views of sexuality. Have you been damaged by previous relationships or abuse? Do you need His healing?
4. How have you portrayed sexuality to your children? Do they view it as a good thing reserved for marriage?
5. Ask the Lord for healthy views of sexually you have conveyed to them.
6. Ask Him about any unhealthy views you have unintentionally conveyed to them.
7. Ask the Lord how He would have you respond to this chapter, for yourself and for your kids.

• • •

staying heart-connected

chapter 17
THE POWER OF GOD TRUMPS THE LAW

> "You Christians have in your keeping a document with enough dynamite in it to blow the whole of civilization to bits, to turn society upside down, to bring peace to this war-torn world. But you read it as if it were just good literature, and nothing else." Mahatma Ghandi

> "Jesus does not offer to make bad people good but to make dead people alive." Ravi Zacharias

> "No one ever drew close to the heart of God by keeping the law." Mark Ford

> "I have simplified the Christian life down to three basic things. Jesus. Jesus. Jesus." Mike Wells

Over the years, I have heard two analogies of the Christian life. Both seem reasonable, yet they make an opposite point. I will present them and you look for the difference.

A Matter of Degrees

In the first story, a plane is traveling from Los Angeles to New York. If the trajectory is off by even a few degrees, the plane will end up in Florida instead of New York. Those few degrees are almost imperceptible at takeoff, but over distance they become thousands of miles. The point is that if you must be extremely careful, because if you are off even a few degrees in your Christian life, you will end up far, far from your destination.

Course-Correction

In the second story, we discover that planes are never flying perfectly straight, but are constantly making adjustments for the wind, slightly left, slightly right, during the entire course of the flight. (This is easy to see in driving even a straight highway, as you constantly adjust the steering wheel.) The point is that in your Christian life, you must make constant adjustments, even course-corrections, to arrive where you intended.

What's Your Course?

These stories both sound plausible, yet they make opposite points. What is the difference between them? One stays on a course without ever compensating for new information, outside influences and input from the other crew. So small mistakes as a parent translate to being thousands of miles off at the end.

The other one is correctable, constantly allowing himself to make changes as needed. He never considers himself beyond hearing the Lord, and he knows the Lord speaks through others as well. If we are not correctable, we are not walking the Christian life.

It's About the Tree of Life

We discussed at length God's call to us to live off the tree of life rather than the tree of knowledge of good and evil. This concept is the crux of loving the Lord with all your heart, soul mind and strength, and loving others as yourself – it is worth another good look as we draw our time together to a close.

We are so prone to living off the tree of knowledge that it takes dynamite just to break through the structure of the law. Then we have to remove all the debris. But I have some ideas why we might live from the tree of knowledge when we have fully available to us the tree of life.

> We are so fond of the list, in fact, that a watching world...considers Christianity to be a Do/Don't list. That breaks my heart.

One big reason is that this concept is not well understood by the Christian community, nor is it taught in our churches. But there's more to it. The truth is, we like a list because a list is predictable and God is not. We like the predictability. To follow a list is more predictable than to submit to an infinitely powerful and utterly uncontrollable God! If I forego the list to follow the living God, I am going to face unpredictable challenges. It's like a job description: if I get a list of my duties, I can evaluate whether to agree to the job. But if the job description says: "Do whatever the boss tells you," then I'd better trust that boss, because I will undoubtedly find myself facing directives I was not expecting. *The real issue here is how much we trust God!*

The list works well for a computer program. But it is not sufficient for growing, living, changing human beings. It is so tempting to make a list to parent by – *these things are okay, these are not okay.* Bookstores are chock full of books about what to do and what not to do. But that is not sufficient if our goal is to train our children to love the Lord with all their heart, soul, mind and strength. We wish it were! We are so fond of the list, in fact, that a watching world – who needs Jesus – considers Christianity to be a Do/Don't list. That breaks my heart.

"Oh yeah, they're the ones who don't dance. They're the ones who wear those things on their heads. They're the ones who don't drink. And don't *cuss* around them."

What a pity that a hurting world, who so badly needs what we have been fortunate enough to find, that that world watches us and boils down our Christianity to a Do/Don't list. What a distortion of what God offers us. Every religion has a Do/Don't list, including the various Christian denominations...and it's all legalism.

People in the world, who would like answers to their questions if they could find them – how are they going to distinguish us from other beliefs? What will draw them? We can't count on the fact that we will deliver that list more sweetly or with a bigger smile on our face. The list condemns (Galatians 3:10).

One of the saddest things for me is when a story breaks about a legalistic, cultish "Christian" sect, because I know the world just uses it as more proof that they don't want any part of Christianity. They don't know that the law is the *opposite* of Jesus. They have no idea that Jesus came to fulfill the law (Matthew 5:17) and to free us from the law (Acts 13:39). They have no understanding that Jesus is a warm, intimate, personal, knowable, loving Being who accepts us exactly as we are, and whose truth is the *ultimate freedom* (John 8:32).

What do Christians have that the rest of the faiths in the world don't? *Jesus! The Tree of Life.* If we try Christianity in our own power, we no longer have Christianity. A watching world (and our own children) want to see Jesus. What else would draw them? No list will draw people. No list will impart life.

> ...doesn't God want us to hear Him *and* follow the law? No!

There is so much more to fulfillment than making sure your kids keep the rules! The *relationship* will go SO much further than anything else. No one ever drew close to the heart of God by keeping the law.

The same thing that will draw unbelievers is the same thing that will keep believers' hearts on the Lord, and is the same thing that we have that no other sect or cult has: *Jesus!* Jesus is the Life of our faith.

Cults and false religions are *masters* of the law. No one does it better. Cults have exhaustive – and exhausting – manmade requirements for approval: behavior, activities, clothing. But cults do not offer Christ. They cannot imitate the life of Christ, and they will not lift up or worship the name of Jesus. Any "religion" that is not about Jesus is wasting its time.

The law is hard to give up because we can't help thinking that if our righteousness does not come from the law, certainly it at least helps it along? In other words, doesn't God want us to hear Him and follow the law? No! Paul tells us the law is like a husband who has died; we are *no longer married to it* (Romans 7:1-6). Paul tells us that the law was our tutor to lead us to Christ. Once we come to Christ, we are no longer under the tutor (Galatians 3:19-25).

Our Bible is so incongruent with the culture, with man's ideas, that Mahatma Ghandi made this observation: "You Christians have in your keeping a document with enough dynamite in it to blow the whole of civilization to bits, to turn society upside down, to bring peace to this war-torn world. But you read it as if it were just good literature, and nothing else."

Ghandi is talking about the power of God, not a to-do list. We know from Jesus, from Paul, and from our long experience, that there is no power in rules outside of the power to point out our need for a Savior. That is their only power and only purpose.

Heartwork

1. Where do you see yourself eating from the tree of life?
2. Where do you see yourself eating from the tree of knowledge of the good and evil?
3. Do you the see that one is about Him and the other is about you?
4. Contemplate Romans 7:1-6 and Galatians 3:19-25.
5. What does God have to tell you at this point?
6. Do you see where you have asked your children to eat from the tree of knowledge?

7. Ask the Lord to provide whatever changes, repentance, and healing are needed.

∙ ∙ ∙

chapter 18
THANK GOD ALMIGHTY WE'RE FREE AT LAST

"Life should NOT be a journey to the grave with the intention of arriving safely in an attractive and well preserved body, but rather to skid in sideways, champagne in one hand - strawberries in the other, body thoroughly used up, totally worn out, and screaming, 'WOO HOO – what a ride!'" Unknown

"Life is either a daring adventure or nothing." Helen Keller

"God relishes surprise. We want lives of simple, predictable ease – smooth, even trails as far as the eye can see – but God likes to go off-road. He provokes us with twists and turns. He places us in predicaments that seem to defy our endurance; and comprehension – and yet don't. By His love and grace, we persevere. The challenges that make our hearts leap and stomachs churn invariably strengthen our faith and grant measures of wisdom and joy we would not experience otherwise." Tony Snow, facing cancer

"So if the Son makes you free, you will be free indeed." John 8:36

Freedom is a Choice

Flying. I love to fly. I don't mean in an airplane. I mean in my dreams. I dream often of flying, and I love it because when I'm flying, I have no fear, no limitations, nothing I can't do. I wake up refreshed, happy... and a little disappointed because it was only a dream. Several years ago, Rob and I went parasailing. Tethered to a boat, we flew along above the sea, above the noise, in peace and quiet and a soft breeze. The experience of flying (parasailing or in my dreams) restores in me a zest for living, a love for adventure, a lifting out of the mundane.

Perhaps that is what people mean when they talk about heaven: they will be able to fly, or sing, or dance, or live in a healed body, or see loved ones – without the weight of this fallen world.

Zest for Living

Try to remember a time when you were little, maybe very little, and you were enthusiastic about life. Weren't you going to save the world? You were going to be the best astronaut/fireman/mother/teacher/explorer that ever lived. And what happened?

Somewhere along the way, you lost that exuberance. More accurately, it was reasoned out of you. Self-doubt seeped in, as you matured and began to live a "normal" life. It does not seem like the abundant life Jesus talked about.

Jesus, and Jesus alone, offers abundant life. John 10:10 tells it all: "The thief comes only to steal and kill and destroy; I came that they may have life, and have it abundantly." You see, Jesus is contrasting what satan wants for us compared to what *He* has for us. The enemy offers death and Jesus offers abundant life. The enemy wants us to cower in fear, and he's very good at getting us to do it. Jesus will overcome our fears in us by the power of God.

Why did Peter have such a crazy idea of getting out of his nice safe boat to start walking on water? I think when he saw *Jesus* do it, something stirred in him. Suddenly he said, "There is so much more to life than what I see! Life is so much fuller and richer than I ever imagined – and Jesus is the reason!"

When Peter got out of that boat, he *did* walk on water! He faltered only when he looked down at his circumstances, at the *reality* that "people don't walk on water." He faltered when his gaze fell from Jesus, who said, "Sure, you can walk on it." What an amazing story. As it's been said: "Only one disciple sank in the Sea of Galilee. *But only one disciple walked on water!*" By taking a risk, we may sink in our circumstances. But only by taking a risk will we walk in the path Jesus has laid out for us.

Every child is full of courage, every child is going to save the world – until the enemy convinces him he's silly, he can't do it, and crushes it out of him. This earth is *bound* by the enemy – who steals, kills and destroys – trying desperately to cheat us of God's abundant life. But greater is He who is in us than he who is in the world. Our job is to remind our kids of who is greater than their doubts and fears, to put courage into them to do what God has for them to do. I don't care if they want to be a astronomer this week and a teacher next week – it doesn't matter. We want to fan the flames of something greater than a safe life. We don't really care what our children end up doing, as long as they know and love the Lord. Our kids need courage to follow the desires God has put in them.

> *...after* Christ bought us and then set us free – and He truly does set us free – the most natural thing in the world is to stick with Him.

I love my relationship with Christ because in Him is the fullest expression of who I am. I love Him because He first loved me. I love that life with Him is about what He has done for me, not what I can do for Him – which is nothing! I love that He is about a love relationship, not rules and regulations. I love the freedom for which Christ has set me free, and the freedom God has given me that keeps me tethered to Him! Isn't that unexpected?

The story goes that Abraham Lincoln was so moved by a slave's plight that he bought the slave at auction so that he could set him free. Upon being set free, the slave said, "You mean I can go anywhere I want?"

"Yes," Lincoln answered.

"I don't have to get your permission?"

"No," he answered.

"Well, then," the now former slave exclaimed, "I'm staying with you!"

Doesn't that thrill your heart?

What may not be immediately obvious is that after Christ bought us and then set us free – and He truly does set us free – the most natural thing in the world is to stick with Him. Why wouldn't we? As Peter asked (John 6:68), where else would we go?

> Our job as parents is to grant our children freedom...

And when we set our kids free, they stick with us. They want to come over for dinner, they call just to talk – *if* we have truly set them free. It occurs naturally. Kids who had to struggle out of their parents' iron grip? They're the ones who say, *Adios, Baby!*

To think that God sent Jesus to die on the cross and rise from the dead to pay for our sins *so that we could become obedient* diminishes His gift to us. He paid to *set us free from the law of sin and death* (Romans 8:2). Obedience is not the goal but a byproduct of the abundant life of Christ.

Our job as parents is to grant our children freedom – freedom to make their own choices and reap their own consequences, to look good or bad for themselves, instead of having to worry about making us look good (as if they don't have enough to figure out already). And we may secretly say, "Well, I'll have both – I'll give them freedom, but I don't want them to make me look bad!"

Well, consider this question: how many people in their free choices "make Jesus look bad"? Plenty. And what does He do? I'll tell you this – He does not correct them to protect His reputation. He lets them do their thing, knowing that their freedom is more important than how they might abuse it. All of us need to let that sink in.

If He is not going to stop us, to preserve His reputation – on whom people's eternal salvation depends – then we don't need to stop our children to preserve *our* reputation – on whom *no one's life depends*. The only way they really get to know Him fully and deeply is in freedom.

Your relationship with your children will shift into friendship. Rob and I always heard that kids have lots of friends and only two parents, and that our job is to be parents, not friends. And that's true… *when they are little*. But people with healthy relationships with their grown children have become friends, absolutely. That parent/child relationship has given way to something richer and more satisfying, as you can now enjoy each other as friends. I don't miss those dependent little ones because they have become my precious and treasured friends!

Teenaged "Jessica" lived with us for a while because her parents were so completely controlling and dysfunctional, and I had the privilege of discipling her. Long after she moved into her own apartment, she would call from time to time for advice.

She said to me one day, "My parents always said they're not supposed to be friends with their kids, but what I need is someone like a friend, but older and wiser that I can ask advice from. I don't need someone to tell me to clean my room anymore. I need someone to listen to me and help me see the road ahead." What an honor it is to help someone see the road ahead.

When a healthy transition has taken place, your young adults are likely to seek out your counsel. You can give it then, as an older and wiser friend. You don't want to continue to guide your children's lives when they're thirty, and you don't want your children taking their heartfelt conversations to friends just because you won't listen dispassionately.

I began this chapter talking about God-given dreams that children bring into the world. So I will conclude with a story about childhood dreams… my dreams.

When I was young, I was going to be married to a wonderful man who cherished me, have beautiful children, and be a famous writer! That lovely dream sustained me through years of a severely dysfunctional home.

But with my family, I didn't stand a chance. Think of the house where raggedy children run in the yard and the street, the house from which you hear yelling and see people coming and going at all hours, the house you watch from across the street, shaking your head and saying, "Oh, those poor children!" That was our house. I was a sweet and quiet girl, but as I said, I didn't stand a chance.

> Wilderness is always rough, but through it God accomplished His purpose of bringing us to the end of ourselves.

Across the street from our house (I discovered years later) lived a Christian family who prayed for us diligently. Early on, the Lord drew me. As far back as I can remember, I prayed. At eleven, I received a small, green *New Testament and Psalms*, and I memorized Psalm 23 – without telling anyone. At fourteen, I learned that Jesus was the Way to God, and I readily accepted.

Throughout high school, I went to Young Life and grew in the Lord, journaling my intimacy with Him in long, hand-written pages as girls are prone to do, asking Him to protect me through college "where so many lose their faith," I wrote. But I did lose my faith. And I walked far away, testing every path to find which way would bring me peace. Yet all along, the Holy Spirit resided in me and would not leave! He directed me, convicted me, and continued to love me. I went through counseling and healing workshops – a path the Lord directed, though I did not realize it.

I even married the wonderful man who cherished me and started having those beautiful children. But the Lord was not satisfied to leave me where I was. I was still praying, still considering myself friendly to Him, but I had no understanding of the life He gave me when I gave my life to Him.

Soon after we married, Rob and I came to a wilderness in our life – financial disaster and many accompanying problems. Wilderness is always rough, but through it God accomplished His purpose of bringing us to the end of ourselves. We discovered that the end of yourself is the best place to be because there, if you are willing, you will find the Lord. Rob accepted Christ (my sister Karin had explained Christ's offer to him ever since we met), and I returned to Christ with all my heart.

In a wonderful church, He fast-tracked us to knowing Him more deeply and falling more madly in love with Him! Our growth has included several more breakings since, and with each has come a deeper love, trust, and abiding in Him. We couldn't be more grateful.

I tell you all this, because I didn't stand a chance. But I did have a prayer.

God, in His infinite kindness, sought me until He caught me.

He put the right people in my life to teach me everything I needed. He allowed me to go wherever I thought I would be satisfied (just like the prodigal son), until I came back to Him. In His kindness, He rescued me from myself (which was poverty). I learned that "it is His kindness that leads us to repentance."

If God could keep track of me through the wilderness, create support for me out of thin air, and bring me into the love relationship I have with Him – He can take care of your teen. Who knows? He may even fulfill their dreams!

You are the parent God provided your teens. You can relax in Him and let Him do what He wanted to do in them all along! Thank Him. Love Him. And rest in Him.

God bless you.

Heartwork

1. Ask the Lord to remind you of dreams you had as a child. However silly or unattainable they may seem now, write them down.
2. Ask the Lord how He has fulfilled any of those dreams; which ones He is fulfilling; which ones are not to be.
3. What have you learned in this journey together?
4. What do you love about your relationship with Christ?

5. How has the Lord deepened your heart-connectedness: To Him? To your children?
6. What are you doing in your time with the Lord to keep you heart-connected?
7. Continue to come to Him for guidance on your children, trust Him to take them where He wants them, and enjoy your God and your family.

• • •

Susan Cottrell is a writer, speaker and teacher. She has been married to Rob, a.k.a. Mr. Wonderful, for more than twenty years, with five children now in their teens and twenties. Susan has homeschooled her kids for ages, minus a handful of years she sent them to charter schools to give herself a much-needed rest and writing time.

Susan is thrilled to release this first book in The Heart-Connected Life series, which focuses on the indwelling life of Christ. Her heart's desire is for people to know Christ and the life He offers them. She also helps her husband in his ministry (hopekids.org) and sings with him when he leads worship. She can be contacted directly at HeartConnectedLife.org